Rise from the Arena: A Gladiator's Guide to Overcoming Life's Greatest Challenges

Rowan X. Adler

Adler Horizons

Rowan X. Adler

Copyright 2024

Introduction: Welcome to the Arena

Picture yourself standing in the centre of an ancient Roman arena. The midday sun bears down relentlessly, the heat radiating off the sand like a furnace. The crowd's roar is deafening, a mixture of anticipation, excitement, and bloodlust. You shift your weight slightly, feeling the grit beneath your feet, the leather of your sandals flexing as you steady yourself. In your hand, a weapon—more familiar now than foreign, but no less heavy.

And then, the gates creak open.

Before you is an opponent, towering and imposing, armed and ready. The arena is unforgiving, a place where survival hinges on your skill, your nerve, and your willingness to rise again, no matter how many times you've been knocked down. In that moment, your heartbeat drowns out the noise. Everything narrows to the next move, the next breath, the next choice.

This might not be your literal life, but in many ways, it mirrors the battles we face every day. Whether you're navigating a challenging career, repairing a fractured relationship, or striving to achieve a long-held dream, you are the gladiator in your own arena. Every day presents a fight, not for life or death, but for meaning, growth, and triumph.

The Arena Awaits

This book is your armour and your guide. Through the story of Rufus, a young gladiator thrust into the harsh world of the arena, you'll learn not only how to survive but how to thrive. Rufus's journey is one of resilience, courage, and transformation—a tale that mirrors the struggles and triumphs we all face. His scars, both seen and unseen, tell a story of battles fought and lessons learned, just as your own challenges shape the person you are becoming.

Your battles may not be fought with swords, but their stakes are no less significant. Whether you're struggling to regain confidence after a setback, navigating an uncertain future, or striving to reach a goal that feels just out of reach, this book will arm you with the tools to face your challenges head-on. Like Rufus, you'll learn to adapt, to fight with honour, and to rise no matter how many times you fall.

The gates are opening. The arena is calling. Are you ready to step into the sands?

Themes of the Gladiator's Journey

At its core, life is a series of battles. Each day, we step into our own arenas, armed with whatever tools we've gathered—our wits, our courage, our skills—and face challenges that test us to our limits. Like the gladiators of old, we are asked to fight not only for survival but for something greater: freedom, identity, and purpose.

Rufus's journey illuminates these themes, reminding us that we, too, can transform struggle into strength and failure into wisdom. Let his lessons inspire you as you prepare to confront the trials in your own life.

Resilience

In the arena, defeat often meant death. Yet every gladiator who fought carried the marks of previous failures—scars that bore witness to battles lost and survived. Resilience is the ability to rise again, to shake off the dust and face the next challenge with unwavering determination.

In modern life, resilience is what allows us to recover from failures—whether it's losing a job, enduring heartbreak, or missing an important opportunity. It is the foundation of every victory, the strength that keeps us moving forward when the odds seem insurmountable.

Discipline

Success in the arena was not a matter of raw talent. It was the result of relentless training—gruelling hours spent sparring with wooden swords, honing reflexes, and mastering technique. Gladiators knew that discipline was their only path to survival.

In our own lives, discipline is just as vital. It is the consistent effort that transforms potential into achievement. Whether you're learning a new skill, building a career, or maintaining meaningful relationships, discipline is the quiet force that drives progress, one small step at a time.

Courage

Courage isn't about the absence of fear; it's about stepping forward despite it. Every gladiator knew fear intimately—the pounding heart, the sweat-drenched palms, the instinct to flee. Yet they chose to fight, to face their opponent head-on.

In life, fear often stands between us and what we desire most. Courage is the bridge that allows us to cross over, to take that first step toward a goal, no matter how daunting it seems.

Adaptability

The arena was unpredictable. No two fights were the same, and every opponent brought unique challenges. Gladiators learned to read their adversaries, to adapt their tactics mid-battle, and to use the terrain to their advantage.

Life, too, is full of unexpected twists. Adaptability—the ability to pivot and adjust to changing circumstances—is an invaluable skill. It allows us to thrive in uncertainty, to see opportunity in adversity, and to find creative solutions when the plan falls apart.

Self-Mastery

True freedom, as the gladiators understood, came not from defeating others but from mastering themselves. The ability to control their emotions, focus their energy, and align their actions with their goals defined their success.

In modern life, self-mastery is the cornerstone of growth. It is the ability to silence self-doubt, to resist distraction, and to channel your efforts toward what truly matters. In mastering yourself, you unlock the potential to master your life.

Opportunism

In the unforgiving world of the arena, every advantage mattered. Gladiators learned to exploit their opponent's weaknesses, to seize fleeting opportunities, and to turn the tide of a fight in their favour.

Opportunism in life is about recognising the moments that can change everything—a chance meeting, a bold decision, a leap of faith—and acting on them. It's about staying alert, taking calculated risks, and making the most of the opportunities that come your way.

Leveraging Relationships

Even in the brutal world of gladiatorial combat, alliances mattered. Trust, mentorship, and camaraderie often made the difference between survival and defeat.

Life, too, is rarely a solo endeavour. Building and nurturing meaningful relationships can provide the strength, guidance, and support needed to thrive in our own arenas.

Your Journey Begins

The lessons of the gladiator's journey are timeless, offering a roadmap for facing life's battles with strength and purpose. As you turn the page, prepare to step into the arena alongside Rufus. His story will inspire you to confront your own challenges with resilience, discipline, courage, and heart.

The gates are opening. The sand is warm beneath your feet. The crowd is waiting. It's time to fight—not for survival, but for greatness.

Are you ready to rise?

The Paradox of the Gladiator in Roman Society

The gladiator was a living contradiction: a figure both despised and adored, enslaved yet celebrated. They occupied a strange space in Roman society, one that reveals much about the culture's values and obsessions.

Revered for Bravery, Yet Seen as Expendable

Gladiators were slaves, prisoners of war, or criminals, stripped of their freedom and thrust into a life of violence. Yet, despite their status, they were admired for their bravery, skill, and resilience. The crowd marvelled at their ability to face death with dignity, cheering them on as if their triumphs could momentarily elevate them from their station. This paradox reflects the Roman fascination with strength and endurance, even when displayed by those they considered beneath them.

Commodification of the Gladiator

Gladiators were not just fighters; they were commodities. Their sweat, thought to have aphrodisiacal properties, was collected and sold as perfume to wealthy patrons. Their images adorned merchandise, from oil lamps to figurines, turning them into symbols of virility and power. In this way, they became both people and products, their very essence commodified for entertainment and profit.

The Spectacle of the Games

The games themselves were a grand display of Roman values. Strength, endurance, and spectacle took centre stage, reinforcing the idea that power and glory were the ultimate pursuits. Gladiatorial combat was more than just entertainment; it was a tool of social cohesion, a way to distract and unite the populace while showcasing the empire's dominance and wealth.

We Are All Gladiators

The world may no longer have arenas filled with sand and roaring crowds, but the battles we face are no less real. Each of us fights in our own way—against external challenges, internal doubts, and the obstacles that stand between us and our dreams. Like the gladiators of ancient Rome, we are called to demonstrate resilience, discipline, courage, and adaptability.

Through the journey of Rufus, this book will show you how to embrace these qualities, turning life's struggles into opportunities for growth and triumph. The lessons of the arena are timeless, and the spirit of the gladiator lives on in all of us. As you read, remember: you, too, are a gladiator, and the battles you face today are the proving ground for the victories of tomorrow.

The gates are opening. The arena awaits. It's time to step forward.

The Gladiator Challenge: Chapter-by-Chapter Format

Introduction to the Challenge

Life is not a spectator sport. Each day brings its battles, and every choice we make pushes us closer to victory—or further from it. Just as Rufus fought his way through the trials of the arena, this book invites you to take on your own challenges, inspired by the lessons of his journey.

This is the *Gladiator Challenge*, a chance for you to step into your metaphorical arena and test your strength, courage, and adaptability. With each chapter, you'll face a challenge rooted in the themes of resilience, discipline, and growth.

This is more than just an intellectual exercise—it's an invitation to action. By participating, you'll bring the lessons of this book to life, creating your own path to triumph. And just like Rufus, you won't be alone. Share your journey, inspire others, and connect with a growing community of modern-day gladiators using the hashtag #GladiatorChallenge.

Are you ready to rise like Rufus? The gates are opening, and the arena is calling. Your first challenge awaits. Let the battle begin!

How the Challenge Works

Each chapter of this book is a stepping stone, presenting a unique lesson from Rufus's life as a gladiator. At the end of every chapter, you'll find a challenge designed to help you apply these insights in your own life. These challenges are simple, practical, and impactful, encouraging you to reflect, take action, and grow stronger with each step.

- Reflect: Start by understanding the lesson from Rufus's story and how it relates to your life.
- Act: Tackle the challenge—whether it's trying something new, overcoming a fear, or reaching out to someone.
- Share: Document your journey on social media using #GladiatorChallenge to inspire others and connect with fellow participants.

These challenges aren't about perfection—they're about progress. Like Rufus, you'll face setbacks, but each step you take will bring you closer to becoming the best version of yourself.

Why Join the Gladiator Challenge?

This challenge is your opportunity to do more than just read about resilience, courage, and growth—you'll embody these qualities. By the end of this journey, you won't just have learned the lessons of the arena; you'll have lived them.

And when you share your journey, you'll inspire others to do the same, creating a ripple effect of strength, determination, and change. Together, we can build a community of modern-day gladiators, ready to face life's challenges with courage and grace.

The first challenge awaits. Are you ready to step forward? It's time to rise, fight, and conquer. Let the Gladiator Challenge begin!

Chapter 1:

Captured – When Life Feels Out of Control

The Smoke of Defeat

The air hung heavy with smoke, acrid and suffocating, mingling with the desperate cries of the conquered. The once-proud city of Sarmizegetusa, the capital of Dacia, was no more. Roman standards flapped triumphantly against a sky darkened with ash, their golden eagles glittering mockingly in the faint sunlight. The sacred hills, which had once whispered tales of heroes and gods, now bore the scars of Rome's relentless conquest.

Rufus knelt in the dirt, his wrists bound tightly with rough rope that cut into his skin. His fiery red hair, now matted with sweat and soot, clung stubbornly to his forehead. Piercing blue eyes, dulled by exhaustion yet still alive with defiance, scanned the chaos around him. His chest rose and fell, each breath a struggle under the weight of humiliation.

He had fought valiantly, a young warrior defending his homeland with the unyielding conviction of youth. But conviction was no match for Trajan's legions. His sword, once an extension of his will, lay shattered. His armour, a proud symbol of his lineage, had been stripped away, leaving him exposed to the mocking gaze of his captors. Around him, others knelt in similar misery, their faces etched with the same grief and despair. The empire's war machine had crushed their spirits, leaving behind the hollow shells of a defeated people.

The March of the Broken

The prisoners were herded through the ruined streets like cattle, prodded forward by the blunt ends of Roman spears. Rufus stumbled, his knees buckling under the weight of fatigue, but he did not fall. His captors took note of him—how could they not? His flaming hair and striking eyes set him apart, a rare gem among the ashes of the fallen.

"Look at this one," sneered a soldier, seizing Rufus by the chin and tilting his face toward the light. "He's got spirit. The arena will break that soon enough."

The words sliced through Rufus's stoic façade, though he refused to show it. He had heard whispers of the gladiators—slaves made to fight for the entertainment of the masses, their lives reduced to spectacle. Was this his future? A life of endless violence, performed for the cheers of the empire that had destroyed his own?

His gaze burned into the soldier's, a silent challenge. The soldier's grin faltered, but he recovered quickly, shoving Rufus forward with a barked order. Even in chains, Rufus would not give them the satisfaction of seeing his despair.

A City in Ruins

As the prisoners were marched toward the city gates, Rufus stole one last look at the only home he had ever known. Sarmizegetusa, the sacred capital, was unrecognisable. The great temples had been reduced to rubble, their once-majestic columns now lying in jagged heaps. Statues of the gods, revered for generations, had been toppled and defiled, their stone faces broken and unseeing. The sacred flames, which had burned eternally to protect their people, were extinguished.

Rufus clenched his fists, the rope digging deeper into his flesh, but he welcomed the pain. It was a reminder that he was still alive. As his captors forced him onward, his thoughts drifted to his family. Had they escaped? Or were they among the lifeless bodies littering the streets? He swallowed hard, suppressing the tears that threatened to fall. Tears would not change anything. They would not bring back his people or his city.

Stripped of Dignity

The days of marching stretched endlessly, each one a blur of exhaustion and pain. Roman soldiers drove them forward mercilessly, their shouts and the occasional crack of a whip a constant reminder of their power. Rufus's feet were blistered, his legs weak from hunger, but it was the humiliation that cut the deepest. He had been a warrior, a defender of his homeland. Now, he was nothing more than a prisoner, an object to be bought and sold.

At night, they were chained together like animals, their only comfort the cold, indifferent gaze of the stars above. Rufus lay awake, his mind racing with plans for escape. But the weight of the chains on his wrists was a constant reminder of his powerlessness. For now, the idea of freedom was a distant dream, obscured by the grim reality of his captivity.

The traders appraised him openly, their eyes lingering on his broad shoulders and muscular build. "This one will fetch a high price," one remarked, gripping Rufus's arm as though he were inspecting livestock. Rufus jerked away, his eyes blazing with fury. The trader laughed. "Ah, he's got fight in him. Good. The crowd loves a fighter."

The Depths of Despair

Rufus was no stranger to pain, but this was something deeper—a hollowing out of the soul. Grief, anger, and despair threatened to consume him entirely. There were moments when he wondered if it would be easier to give up, to let the relentless tide of misery drag him under. What was the point of survival when everything that gave life meaning had been taken from him?

Yet, in the darkest moments, a spark of defiance flickered. One night, lying on the cold ground, he stared up at the stars, their light piercing through the darkness. He thought of the stories his father had told him, of heroes who had faced impossible odds and emerged stronger for it. "Survive," he whispered, his voice barely audible. If he could do nothing else, he would endure.

A Name and a Future

The Romans had given him a name: Rufus. It was not his true name—it was a brand, a label meant to strip him of his identity. But to Rufus, it became something else. A reminder that his captors could bind his body, but not his spirit. The fire within him still burned, and it would guide him through whatever trials lay ahead.

As the caravan approached its destination, Rufus began to study his surroundings with a sharp eye. He watched the guards, noting their routines and weaknesses. He memorised the terrain, searching for potential escape routes. The arena might await him, but if Rufus had his way, he would meet it on his own terms.

For now, he would wait. He would endure. And when the moment came, he would rise. The battle for his freedom was far from over.

Captured – When Life Feels Out of Control

The collapse of Rufus's world is more than just a tale of defeat; it's a story of transformation, reminding us that adversity is an inevitable part of life. What defines us is not the obstacles we face, but the way we choose to respond to them. When life feels out of control, embracing the moment with resilience and a willingness to adapt can lead to profound growth.

1. Accept the Reality of Setbacks

Life's challenges often hit us like a sudden storm—unexpected, overwhelming, and out of our control. Our first instinct might be to deny their existence or wish them away. But just as Rufus couldn't undo the fall of his homeland or the chains that bound him, we, too, must face reality head-on. Acceptance is not about surrendering to defeat; it's about acknowledging the truth so we can begin the process of healing and rebuilding.

Think of a ship caught in rough seas. The captain doesn't curse the waves or ignore the storm. Instead, he adjusts their sails, understanding that the only way forward is through. Similarly, acknowledging life's challenges gives us the clarity to navigate them.

- **Practical Step**: Reflect on a challenge you've faced recently. Write down what you're resisting and consider why. Then, list one action that signals acceptance—whether it's having an honest conversation, making a plan, or simply allowing yourself to feel your emotions without judgment.

---

2. Reframe Challenges as Opportunities

When Rufus's identity as a proud Dacian warrior was stripped away, he had two choices: let his loss define him or use it as an opportunity to grow. His captivity, though devastating, gave him the chance to adapt, endure, and eventually rise as a gladiator whose strength inspired others.

In our lives, challenges often arrive disguised as failure or loss. A career setback might be the push we need to pivot toward something more fulfilling. A difficult relationship might teach us boundaries and self-worth. Reframing doesn't mean ignoring pain; it means asking, "What can I learn from this?" and "How can I emerge stronger?"

- **Real-World Anecdote**: Hugh Dowding in the Battle of Britain

Hugh Dowding faced not only the overwhelming military challenge of the Luftwaffe during the Battle of Britain but also personal and professional setbacks that tested his resolve.

A Serious Setback: Political and Peer Criticism

As the Battle of Britain raged, Dowding's strategic decisions, such as prioritising defensive tactics over offensive bombing raids, earned him the ire of some of his peers and political figures. He faced accusations of being overly cautious and was criticised for his firm stance on conserving resources. In one of the most dramatic setbacks, after leading Fighter Command through its most perilous hours, Dowding was abruptly removed from his position in November 1940.

How He Reacted

Instead of lashing out or descending into bitterness, Dowding maintained his dignity. He focused on the legacy of what he had achieved—preserving the "Few" pilots who turned the tide of the war and demonstrating the importance of strategic planning. While his removal was undoubtedly a blow, Dowding later reflected that his contributions during the battle spoke for themselves. He showed that even in professional setbacks, staying true to one's principles and long-term goals can leave a lasting impact.

Dowding's ability to remain steadfast in the face of adversity serves as a powerful example of reframing challenges as opportunities. His innovations in radar and command systems became foundational for modern air defence strategies, and his leadership inspired countless others—even if his recognition came long after his dismissal.

- **Practical Step**: Identify a recent challenge and ask yourself:

1. What lesson can I learn from this?
2. How might this situation push me toward growth or a new opportunity?

---

3. Focus on Survival as the First Victory

In the chaos of losing everything, Rufus didn't aim for grand victories; he focused on surviving each day. Survival wasn't just about existing—it was an act of defiance against despair. Each small triumph, like enduring another march or studying his captors, laid the foundation for his eventual freedom.

When life feels overwhelming, survival becomes our most immediate goal. Sometimes, that means focusing on one manageable task—making a phone call, taking a walk, or even just getting through the day.

- **Real-World Anecdote**: Consider the story of Aron Ralston, the mountaineer who became trapped by a boulder in Utah. Faced with seemingly insurmountable odds, he broke his survival into small, actionable steps, ultimately saving his life. His story reminds us that small victories build momentum.
- **Practical Step**: Each morning, write down one small action you can take to "survive" the day—a task that feels achievable and meaningful. By the evening, reflect on how that action helped you move forward.

Practical Exercises: Building Resilience

Here are three ways to strengthen your resilience and find clarity when life feels out of control:

1. **Reflect on a Moment of Loss or Failure**
   - Write about a time when life felt chaotic or overwhelming.
     - What happened?
     - How did it affect you emotionally and mentally?
     - How did you adapt—or how could you have adapted differently?
   - This reflection helps you process emotions and learn from past experiences.
2. **Write About Growth Through Acceptance**
   - Describe a time when accepting a difficult reality led to growth.
     - Did it teach you patience, courage, or adaptability?
     - What lessons did you carry forward?
   - If you're struggling to accept something now, write down one step you can take today to begin embracing it.

3. **Start a Resilience Journal**

- Document daily wins, no matter how small:
  - "I managed a difficult conversation."
  - "I finished a task I was dreading."
  - "I found five minutes of calm."
- Over time, this journal will remind you of your strength and progress, even in the toughest times.

Closing Thought

Rufus's journey from captured warrior to resilient gladiator wasn't about immediate triumph—it was about enduring, adapting, and rising, one small step at a time. In the Roman arena, freedom wasn't handed to gladiators; it had to be earned. A rudis, a simple wooden sword, was given to signify a gladiator's release from bondage. It wasn't just a symbol of freedom—it was proof of strength, resilience, and the courage to endure.

In your own life, remember that setbacks don't define you. What matters is how you face them. Accept, reframe, and take that first step toward building your own arena of strength. The rudis of freedom is within your reach; you just have to claim it.

Joke:

Why did the gladiator never feel embarrassed about falling in the arena?

Because he always got back up and called it a tactical roll.

The Gladiator Challenge: Rise from the Storm

Reflection Task: Share a moment when life felt chaotic or overwhelming. How did you regain control, or what small step helped you move forward? Post it with #GladiatorChallenge and #SurvivalBegins.

Action Task: Start a resilience journal. Write one thing you're grateful for today that gives you the strength to endure.

Remember:
Every small act of survival is a triumph. Every lesson learned is a step forward. Like Rufus, you have the power to endure, adapt, and rise. Your journey doesn't have to inspire the world—it just has to inspire you.

The arena awaits. Will you step forward?

Chapter 2:

The Chains of Despair – Facing Initial Defeat

The Gates of Submission

The iron gates of the gladiators' school, the ludus, groaned as they swung open, revealing a grim, almost otherworldly scene. The air was heavy with the acrid scent of sweat, blood, and the faint metallic tang of old weapons. The yard was alive with activity: men sparring with wooden swords, others running weighted laps under the unrelenting bark of orders, and a few sprawled on the ground, too exhausted to rise. This was not a place of ambition or hope. It was a crucible of survival, where men were broken, reshaped, and forged into weapons.

Rufus stumbled forward, the iron chain around his neck pulling taut as he joined the line of new recruits. The Roman guards shoved the group into place with a lack of ceremony that spoke volumes about their perceived worth. Before him stood the lanista, the head trainer of the school, a towering figure with a face as hard as the stones lining the courtyard. The lanista's eyes scanned Rufus with the detached appraisal of a butcher inspecting livestock.

"He'll do," the lanista said, his voice cold and final, as though Rufus's life had already been signed away. It had.

The New Reality

Life in the ludus was merciless. The day began before dawn, with the clanging of iron rods on wooden posts and the trainers' shouts echoing across the yard. There was no room for delay, no tolerance for weakness. The newly acquired slaves were stripped of individuality, their existence now defined by the schedule imposed upon them.

The training was as gruelling as the march that had brought Rufus to this place. Weighted runs left his legs trembling, and relentless sparring drills with wooden swords reduced his palms to blistered agony. The rods of the trainers were quick to punish any hesitation or misstep, driving the recruits to move faster, hit harder, and endure longer. Rufus's body, once a testament to his warrior heritage, ached in ways he had never imagined. But the physical pain was bearable compared to the assault on his spirit.

He was no longer Rufus, the Dacian warrior defending his homeland. Here, he was no one. He was nothing but a body to be honed and used for the entertainment of others.

The Crushing Weight of Despair

As the days dragged on, Rufus observed the faces around him. Some were young and filled with a glimmer of defiance, much like his own. Others bore the hollow look of men who had endured this life for years. They moved like automatons, executing their drills with grim precision but no spark of life.

One figure stood out—a gaunt, scarred man named Magnus, who had once been a legend in the arena. Now, he was a shadow of that glory, his movements slow and laboured, his body bent under the weight of age and injury. Watching Magnus struggle, mocked and beaten by the trainers, Rufus felt the cold fingers of realization gripping his mind. This was his future. The ludus had no room for the weak. It would forge him into a weapon or discard him like broken steel.

Each night, Rufus lay on the hard ground, staring up at the stars. The cold seeped into his bones, a bitter reminder of his isolation. The weight of his loss—his homeland, his family, his freedom—pressed down on him, suffocating and unrelenting. There were moments when he thought of giving up, of letting the trainers' rods and the endless drills take him to the point of no return.

But somewhere deep inside, a small ember of defiance still burned.

A Glimmer of Humanity

Not every moment was consumed by despair. Occasionally, amid the brutality, there were glimpses of camaraderie. During one particularly punishing drill, when Rufus's legs threatened to give out beneath him, a fellow recruit silently passed him a waterskin. Another day, after a sparring match left him bleeding and battered, a man named Felix offered him a piece of bread.

"Keep standing, Dacian," Felix said with a crooked grin. "The sand loves the stubborn."

These acts of kindness were rare, but they were enough to remind Rufus that even in a place designed to strip away humanity, some vestiges of it remained. The gladiators found ways to resist their dehumanisation—turning drills into competitions, sharing crude jokes about the trainers, or simply sitting together in silence, drawing strength from each other's presence.

Rufus began to understand that survival here wasn't just about strength or skill. It was about finding those small moments of connection and holding onto them like a lifeline.

The Mentor and the Rival

Rufus's journey in the ludus took a sharp turn when Magnus, the veteran gladiator he had watched with a mix of pity and dread, approached him after a training session.

"You've got fire, Dacian," Magnus said, his voice raspy but steady. "But fire can burn out quick if you're careless. Use your head, not just your sword."

Magnus's advice was harsh but valuable. Over the following days, he began to offer Rufus pointers during sparring drills, correcting his stance, teaching him how to conserve energy, and pointing out weaknesses in his opponents. Magnus was no friend—he had long since lost the capacity for that—but he was a guide, shaping Rufus into something stronger.

Not everyone was so supportive. A recruit named Varro, a lean, wiry man with quick reflexes and an arrogant smirk, took an immediate dislike to Rufus. During a paired drill, Varro deliberately tripped him, sending him sprawling into the dirt.

"Careful, redhead," Varro sneered. "The sand's hungry, and it'll eat you alive if you let it."

Rufus picked himself up slowly, wiping the grit from his face. *"Good thing I've got someone like you to remind me,"* he muttered.

Yet he bit back his anger, knowing a fight now would only earn him punishment. But the tension between the two simmered, promising future conflict.

Enduring and Learning

As the weeks passed, Rufus adapted. He began to move with more confidence, his strikes growing sharper, his endurance greater. The lessons from Magnus, the camaraderie with men like Felix, and even the animosity from Varro fuelled his determination. He was no longer just surviving—he was learning, growing, becoming.

The ludus was a crucible, and Rufus could feel himself being forged. His body bore the marks of the process—blisters, bruises, and scars—but it was his mind that was changing the most. He no longer thought of himself as a prisoner. He was something more, something stronger.

The chains of despair still clung to him, but they were beginning to loosen. Rufus wasn't broken. He was becoming a gladiator.

Historical Context: Life in the Ludus

The daily life of a gladiator in ancient Rome was nothing short of a battle for survival. Training regimens were brutal and unrelenting, designed to turn men into instruments of war. Gladiators spent hours sparring with wooden swords and shields, their movements scrutinised and corrected by trainers who demanded perfection.

Meals were functional, consisting mostly of barley porridge and legumes, meant to build strength and endurance rather than provide comfort. Injuries were treated with care, not out of kindness, but because every gladiator represented an investment. They were commodities, and their value depended on their ability to fight and entertain.

Even beyond the arena, gladiators were commodified. Their sweat, believed to have aphrodisiacal properties, was collected and sold to wealthy patrons. Their images adorned merchandise, turning them into symbols of power and virility. Yet for all the reverence they inspired, gladiators remained slaves, their fates dictated by the whims of their owners.

Reflections of Resilience

For Rufus, the ludus was both a prison and a proving ground. It tested his body, his mind, and his spirit in ways he could never have imagined. Yet, even in the darkest moments, he found the will to endure. He might have been treated as a commodity, but within him burned a determination to rise above his circumstances.

The chains of despair were heavy, but they would not define him. If the ludus sought to break him, it would first have to face the fire within. Rufus resolved to survive, not just for himself, but for the memory of his homeland and the hope of a future beyond the arena.

In the harsh confines of the ludus, he began to learn that even in the face of defeat, there was strength to be found in endurance—and sometimes, in the bonds we forge with those who share our struggles.

Self-Help Lessons: The Chains of Despair – Facing Initial Defeat

Rufus stood in the middle of the training yard, sweat dripping from his brow as the unforgiving sun blazed overhead. Around him, the sound of clashing wood and grunts of exertion filled the air. The trainers barked commands with unrelenting ferocity, their rods snapping against the backs of those who faltered. The weight of his chains and the scars from his capture were constant reminders of how far he had fallen. The proud Dacian warrior was gone. In his place stood a man struggling to find his footing in a world that demanded both submission and strength.

Yet, for all the brutality of the ludus, Rufus found himself grappling with something more insidious than the physical pain: despair. Each failed drill, each reprimand, seemed to chip away at his spirit. What hope could there be in a place designed to strip men of their humanity?

But despair didn't win. Not entirely. Somewhere in the depths of Rufus's soul, a small ember of defiance burned. It wasn't a grand rebellion or an immediate transformation. It was a quiet resolution to survive—not by leaps and bounds, but by small, steady steps.

Mindset is Key

Rufus's turning point came not in a triumphant victory but in a moment of clarity. As the lanista sneered at him during yet another faltered drill, Rufus realized something: the man's words could only break him if he allowed them to. Survival in the ludus wasn't just about brute strength or flawless performance—it was about endurance. Every strike of the rod, every barked insult, every aching muscle was an invitation to give up. But Rufus refused to accept it.

He began focusing on what he could control. The weight of his chains? He couldn't change that. The unforgiving drills? He couldn't escape them. But his mindset—his decision to put one foot in front of the other, to treat each drill as an opportunity rather than a punishment—that was his to shape.

In our own lives, the same principle applies. Life will throw challenges our way, many of which we can't control. But what we can control is how we respond to those challenges. Like Rufus, we can choose to see each difficulty not as a wall but as a stepping stone.

Small Victories Build Momentum

In the world of the ludus, small victories were all Rufus had to hold onto. The first time he finished a drill without stumbling. The rare nod of approval from the lanista. The simple piece of bread Felix offered him after a particularly brutal day. These moments weren't monumental, but they were enough to keep him going.

Rufus began to see these small wins as building blocks. Each one, no matter how minor, added to his growing sense of resilience. He started marking them in his mind, replaying them at night when the weight of despair threatened to creep back in. "Today," he would think, "I didn't fall. Today, I held my ground."

Small victories are the foundation of progress. In our lives, they remind us that even when the bigger picture feels overwhelming, we are capable of moving forward. These moments don't have to be grand or dramatic. Sometimes, just getting through the day is enough.

Practical Exercise: Building Strength Through Small Wins

1. Identify One Small Action

Think of a challenge you're currently facing. Now, break it into smaller, manageable pieces. Choose just one action you can take today to move forward.

- **If you're feeling overwhelmed by a long to-do list**, pick one priority task and focus solely on completing it.
- **If you're struggling emotionally**, commit to one small act of self-care, like taking a walk, journaling, or calling a friend.

Write it down and commit to doing it. The goal isn't to solve everything—it's to take the first step.

---

2. Write Down Three Small Wins

At the end of your day or week, take a moment to reflect. What are three things you accomplished, no matter how small?

- Did you overcome the urge to procrastinate on something important?
- Did you take a step, however small, toward a personal goal?
- Did you find a moment of joy or connection amid the chaos?

Write these wins down in a journal or app. Over time, you'll create a record of your progress—proof that you're moving forward even when it feels like you're standing still.

---

3. Build a Habit of Celebration

Pick one of your small wins and celebrate it in a way that feels meaningful to you.

- Share your success with someone who supports you.
- Treat yourself to something simple but enjoyable, like your favourite snack or a quiet moment of relaxation.
- Pause to reflect on what this win says about your resilience and strength.

Celebrating these small victories reinforces the behaviours that lead to progress. It's not just about feeling good in the moment—it's about creating a mindset that recognises and values growth.

Rufus's Journey: The Power of Small Steps

Rufus didn't become a gladiator overnight. His path from despair to resilience was paved with small victories. Each step forward, no matter how minor, was a triumph against the odds. In your own life, remember that progress doesn't always have to be dramatic. Sometimes, it's the quiet wins—the finished task, the moment of calm, the act of kindness—that carry you forward.

Your chains may feel heavy today, but with each small step, each small victory, you loosen their grip. Progress is happening, even when it feels slow. Trust in the power of those small wins. The arena awaits, and you're stronger than you think.

Joke:

Why did the gladiator refuse to give up?

He couldn't stand the thought of throwing in the towel—it was part of his armour.

The Gladiator Challenge: Celebrate Your Wins

Daily Challenge: Identify one small task you can accomplish today that will bring you closer to a larger goal. Complete it and share your win with #SmallVictories #GladiatorChallenge.

Visual Task: Post a photo of something that represents your victory—a completed task, a meaningful object, or a personal milestone.

Remember: Small victories are the building blocks of resilience. With each one, you're forging the strength to face bigger battles ahead. Celebrate them, cherish them, and use them to keep moving forward. Your arena awaits—step in with confidence.

Chapter 3:

Forging Discipline – Turning Weakness into Strength

The Sand, the Sweat, and the Sword

The training yard of the ludus was a battlefield in its own right. The relentless sun bore down on the gladiators, turning the sand beneath their feet into a blistering furnace. The air was alive with the grunts of effort, the rhythmic thud of wooden swords against shields, and the occasional crack of the lanista's rod—a sharp reminder of the consequences of failure.

Rufus stood among the recruits, his chest heaving and his grip on the training sword unsteady. His arms felt like lead, trembling from the endless repetitions that filled the hours of his days. Across from him, the lanista, wiry and sharp-eyed, watched his every move. His voice cut through the air like a whip.

"Again!" the lanista barked, his tone as merciless as the drills themselves. "The arena doesn't reward weakness. It punishes it. Again!"

Rufus gritted his teeth, forcing his body into motion. He lunged forward, but his strike was off-balance, the wooden blade skimming past the target with a hollow thud. The lanista sneered, his expression a mixture of disdain and disappointment.

"Pathetic," he said, his words biting deep. "The crowd won't cheer for a fool. They'll jeer while your blood soaks the sand."

The sting of those words wasn't just in their delivery—it was in the truth behind them.

The Relentless Grind

Each day began in darkness, the horn's shrill cry piercing the predawn stillness. Training was a ceaseless cycle of physical torment and mental endurance, designed to break the weak and mould the strong. The recruits were put through their paces with punishing drills: endless sword strikes, gruelling runs with weights strapped to their backs, and sparring sessions that often ended with someone sprawled in the dirt.

For Rufus, the demands of gladiatorial training were unlike anything he had faced before. As a warrior, he had relied on instinct and strength, but the lanista's methods demanded precision, discipline, and control. Each misstep earned a cutting remark or a sharp rap from the rod.

"You think brute strength will save you?" the lanista snarled during a morning drill, watching Rufus stumble through a sequence of strikes. "Strength is worthless without discipline. Learn to master your body, your mind, and your fear—or you'll be dead before the crowd even knows your name."

Those words echoed in Rufus's mind long after the day's training had ended. Lying on his pallet that night, his body aching and his pride battered, he replayed the lanista's voice over and over. Discipline. Control. Mastery. If he couldn't learn those things, he might as well be digging his own grave.

Turning Point: Small Triumphs

The early days were an unbroken string of failures. Rufus's strikes were wild, his footwork clumsy, and his endurance lagged behind the others. Each stumble felt like a nail in the coffin of his pride, a constant reminder of how far he had fallen from the warrior he once was.

"Congratulations, Dacian," Felix had remarked after one particularly embarrassing tumble. "You've managed to make tripping over your own feet look like a battle strategy."

But progress, he began to realize, wasn't a sudden transformation—it was a slow, relentless grind.

One afternoon, during a sparring session, Rufus found himself paired with Felix, a seasoned gladiator whose skill was matched only by his penchant for sharp humour. The lanista, as always, wasted no opportunity to undermine Rufus's confidence.

“Try not to embarrass yourself, Dacian,” he muttered as Felix raised his training sword with a smirk.

Felix leaned in, grinning, and added, *“If it helps, just pretend I’m a tree. You seem to have a knack for fighting those.”*

The words stung, but instead of shrinking under their weight, Rufus felt something shift inside him. A stubborn determination sparked to life.

As Felix lunged forward, Rufus’s instincts kicked in. He raised his sword just in time, the wooden blades colliding with a satisfying crack. Felix grinned, clearly surprised.

“Well, I’ll be damned,” Felix said, stepping back with a twinkle in his eye. “He’s awake, boys!”

They circled each other, exchanging blows. Rufus’s movements weren’t perfect, but they carried a new focus, a steadiness that hadn’t been there before.

When the spar ended, Rufus was still on his feet—a small victory, but a victory nonetheless. Felix slapped him on the back, grinning.
“I’m impressed, Dacian,” Felix said. “That’s the first time you didn’t look like you were apologizing to your opponent.”

For the first time, the lanista’s face betrayed a flicker of approval.
“You’re learning,” he said, his tone still gruff but lacking the usual bite. “Don’t stop now.”

Rufus allowed himself a brief moment of satisfaction. *Maybe tomorrow, I’ll figure out how to stop the sword from feeling like a log. One miracle at a time.*

Forging Strength from Weakness

That moment was a turning point. For the first time since his capture, Rufus felt a spark of pride—not in his past, but in the progress he was making now. It wasn’t about perfection. It was about persistence, about chipping away at the mountain of his own inadequacies one swing of the sword at a time.

Each day, he pushed himself harder. His strikes grew sharper, his footwork steadier, his endurance greater. He began to anticipate his opponent's moves during sparring, using not just brute force but strategy. The bruises and blisters that had once been badges of humiliation now felt like marks of progress.

During one particularly gruelling drill, Rufus managed to disarm his partner—a feat that earned him a rare nod from the lanista. Felix, watching from the sidelines, clapped him on the back.

"Not bad, Dacian," Felix said with a grin. "Maybe one day you'll even give me a challenge."

Rufus grinned back, his chest swelling with a mixture of exhaustion and pride. The lanista's voice rang out again, summoning them back to the line, but this time, Rufus didn't feel the usual dread.

The Mental Shift

Lying on his pallet that night, Rufus stared at the wooden beams above him, his thoughts surprisingly clear. He still missed his homeland, still felt the weight of all he had lost, but something had changed. The despair that had once threatened to crush him had given way to a quiet determination.

He wasn't just surviving anymore. He was fighting—not just against his captors, but against the weakness within himself. The lanista's harsh words no longer felt like insults; they felt like challenges, goading him to be better.

"I will rise," Rufus whispered to himself, the words a vow as much as a promise. He would become stronger. He would master himself. And when the time came, he would fight not just to survive but to reclaim his life.

The sands of the arena awaited, but Rufus knew one thing for certain: he would meet them on his own terms.

Historical Context: The Forge of the *Ludus*

The life of a gladiator was defined by relentless training. At the core of this was the use of wooden swords, known as *rudii*, which allowed gladiators to practice strikes and defences without the risk of serious injury. These drills were repeated endlessly, honing both muscle memory and mental discipline.

Physical conditioning was equally rigorous. Weighted runs, climbing exercises, and strength training were staples of the regimen, designed to build stamina and resilience. The diet was simple but effective, consisting mainly of barley porridge, legumes, and vegetables to ensure strength and endurance. Injuries were common but treated with care, as a gladiator's value lay in their ability to fight.

The lanista was a central figure in this world, equal parts teacher and enforcer. While they were often harsh and demanding, their primary goal was to prepare gladiators for the brutal realities of the arena. A well-trained gladiator brought prestige to the school—and profit to the lanista.

Triumph Amidst the Grind

Weeks turned into months, and Rufus's transformation became evident. His strikes now carried precision, his footwork flowed like a dance, and his endurance allowed him to spar for longer periods without faltering. One day, during a particularly gruelling drill, he completed the course without a single mistake—a feat that earned him a rare nod of approval from the lanista.

"You've earned your place here, Rufus," the lanista said, his tone begrudgingly respectful. "But don't think for a moment that you're ready for the arena. Discipline isn't something you achieve—it's something you maintain. Every day."

The words stayed with Rufus. He knew his journey was far from over, but for the first time, he felt the stirrings of pride in his progress. His body, once battered and weak, now felt like a weapon—a tool he could wield with purpose and precision.

More importantly, his mind had begun to shift. The despair that had gripped him upon his arrival was giving way to determination. He might be a slave in chains, but in the *ludus*, he was forging something unbreakable: himself.

The arena loomed in the distance, but Rufus knew he was no longer the man who had stumbled through the gates on his first day. He was becoming something more—a gladiator.

Self-Help Lessons: Forging Discipline – Turning Weakness into Strength

The sun blazed mercilessly over the training yard, its heat baking the sand and the sweat-drenched gladiators who toiled within it. Rufus stood in the centre of the chaos, his wooden sword trembling slightly in his grip as the lanista shouted commands that cut through the air like a whip.

"Again!" the lanista roared, his eyes narrowing at Rufus. "You think you'll survive with that weak swing? A toddler could do better!"

Rufus clenched his jaw and raised the sword, his arms screaming in protest. His body ached from endless drills, his legs wobbled from weighted runs, and his mind buzzed with the memory of every mistake he'd made since arriving at the ludus. He wanted to scream, to throw the sword down and collapse in the shade. But he didn't. Instead, he tightened his grip, planted his feet, and swung again.

The wooden blade struck the practice dummy with a satisfying thud. It wasn't perfect, but it was progress. And for Rufus, progress was everything.

Discipline Creates Freedom

Rufus's journey through the unforgiving routines of the ludus was more than just physical conditioning—it was a lesson in the transformative power of discipline. At first, he bristled against the rigidity of the drills, the endless repetition that left his muscles burning and his spirit weary. But as the weeks passed, something shifted. The very routines he had resented began to give him a sense of control, a rhythm that steadied him in the chaos of the ludus.

Each swing of the sword, each lap around the yard, was a step toward mastery. And with mastery came freedom—the freedom to act without hesitation, to trust his instincts when the stakes were highest. Discipline, Rufus realized, wasn't a cage. It was the key to unlocking his potential.

In our own lives, discipline plays a similar role. While it may feel restrictive at first, creating structure and habits actually frees us from the chaos of indecision and the weight of unpreparedness. Whether it's building a career, nurturing a relationship, or pursuing a personal goal, discipline provides the foundation for meaningful progress.

Consistent Effort Beats Talent

Rufus wasn't the strongest or the fastest in the ludus. His early days were marked by awkward movements and stinging failures. Other gladiators seemed to master techniques effortlessly, their natural talent shining in every drill. But Rufus had something they didn't: grit.

Day after day, he showed up. He swung his sword until his arms felt like lead. He ran until his legs gave out. He endured the lanista's biting remarks and the sneers of his peers. And slowly, almost imperceptibly, he began to improve. His strikes grew sharper, his footwork steadier. The lanista, once quick to criticise, began nodding in approval.

This transformation wasn't born of raw talent—it was the result of relentless effort. Rufus's progress was a testament to the power of persistence, a reminder that showing up consistently can outshine even the brightest natural ability.

In your own arena, you don't need to be the most talented to succeed. What matters is your willingness to put in the work, day after day, even when progress feels slow. Discipline turns potential into power, one small step at a time.

Practical Exercise: Building Discipline in Your Own Arena

1. Develop a Daily Habit Tracker

Start small. Choose one area of your life where you'd like to improve—whether it's your health, career, or personal growth. Then, identify a simple habit you can practice daily to make progress in that area.

- **Examples:**
  - Drink a glass of water each morning to kickstart your day with hydration.
  - Spend 10 minutes reading a book to expand your knowledge.
  - Do a 5-minute stretch or workout to improve your fitness.

Create a habit tracker to record your progress. You can use a notebook, a spreadsheet, or a habit-tracking app. Each time you complete the habit, mark it on your tracker. Seeing those marks add up will motivate you to keep going.

---

2. Set a Weekly Goal

Discipline thrives on structure, so give your new habit a clear purpose by setting a weekly goal.

- **Examples:**
  - "I will walk for 15 minutes every day this week."
  - "I will write 300 words for my project each day."

o "I will spend 5 minutes reflecting on my day before bed."

At the end of the week, evaluate your progress. Ask yourself:

- What worked well?
- What challenges did I face?
- How can I adjust to keep improving?

Remember, the goal isn't perfection—it's consistency. Missing a day doesn't mean failure. What matters is your commitment to get back on track.

---

3. Build a Momentum Map

To visualise your progress, create a "momentum map." Draw a path with milestones that represent your larger goal. Each milestone should be tied to a specific habit or achievement.

- **Example:**

o Goal: Run a 5K race.

o Milestones:

1. Walk 10 minutes daily for the first week.
2. Jog for 5 minutes daily in week two.
3. Complete a 1-mile run by week three.

As you reach each milestone, mark it on your map and celebrate the progress. Seeing your journey laid out visually reinforces the idea that small steps lead to big results.

Rufus's Journey: Discipline as Freedom

The endless drills and gruelling routines of the ludus transformed Rufus from a struggling captive into a skilled gladiator. Each day, each swing of the sword, built not just his strength but his confidence. Discipline gave him the tools to survive and, eventually, to thrive.

In your own life, discipline can do the same. By committing to daily habits and consistent effort, you build a foundation for success. Your challenges may not involve wooden swords or blistering heat, but the principles remain the same. Show up. Do the work. Trust the process.

The arena awaits. What will you build with the power of discipline?

Joke:

Why did the gladiator refuse to give up?

He couldn't stand the thought of throwing in the towel—it was part of his armour.

The Gladiator Challenge: Commit to Your Habit

Discipline Tracker: Create and share a simple daily habit you want to build (e.g., exercise, journaling, learning). Post your tracker template or your plan with #ForgeDiscipline.

Community Task: Tag a friend or accountability partner and challenge them to build their own routine alongside you.

Final Reflection

Rufus didn't transform overnight. His journey was a series of small, disciplined steps that added up to significant change. The same is true for you. Each day you show up for yourself, you're building the strength and resilience needed to overcome life's challenges.

Remember: every habit you cultivate, every effort you make, is a step toward freedom—the freedom to live life on your terms. Your arena awaits. How will you prepare?

Chapter 4:
Brotherhood in the Arena – Building Alliances

The Unspoken Battles

The training yard of the ludus was more than a proving ground for combat skills; it was a crucible for relationships. Every sparring session, shared meal, and whispered conversation carried an undercurrent of strategy. Alliances were formed and tested, trust was given and broken, and every interaction carried the weight of survival.

Rufus observed these dynamics with wary detachment. He stood apart, his meals eaten in silence as he studied the camaraderie that seemed to flourish despite their circumstances. Laughter often punctuated the air, jarring in its incongruity. How could these men—captives like himself—find joy in such a grim existence?

Among them was Felix, a wiry gladiator with a quick wit and an irrepressible grin. Felix moved through the group like an uninvited guest at a feast, teasing and cajoling in equal measure. He had nicknamed Rufus "the silent Dacian," a title that carried equal parts challenge and invitation.

"Careful, Silent One," Felix said one evening as Rufus sat alone. "If you stay too quiet, they'll start thinking you've got secrets worth keeping."

Rufus didn't answer, but a faint smirk betrayed his amusement. It was the first crack in the walls he had so carefully built.

Camaraderie in the Shadows

Over time, Rufus began to see the small, vital threads of solidarity woven through the harsh fabric of ludus life. During drills, a steadying hand might appear on his shoulder when his stance wavered. After sparring, a piece of bread or an encouraging word often found its way to him.

Felix was at the centre of much of it, his antics a strange balm for the relentless grind. One particularly gruelling day, as the recruits sat slumped over their meagre bowls of barley porridge, Felix nudged Rufus with an exaggerated look of pity. "You've got the swing of a drunk farmer," Felix said, grinning, "but at least your sword's pointing in the right direction now. Improvement's improvement, eh?"

Rufus, his appetite for sarcasm finally outrunning his exhaustion, raised an eyebrow.

"And your shield?" he replied, voice dry but tinged with amusement. "Perhaps one day it'll stop leaking hits like an old wine barrel."

Felix's laugh rang out, loud and unapologetic, drawing the attention of the other gladiators.

"Fair point, Dacian," Felix said, wiping his mouth theatrically. "I'll aim for fewer holes tomorrow. But if I start doing too well, don't be jealous. Not everyone can be as mediocre as you."

It was a moment of levity in a place that thrived on severity, and it didn't go unnoticed. Around them, a few other gladiators smirked, some even chuckling softly. The laughter was fleeting, but it carried a weight that words couldn't touch—proof that even here, humanity hadn't been entirely crushed.

These exchanges chipped away at Rufus's isolation. He began to see that camaraderie wasn't a weakness; it was a tool, a weapon as sharp as any sword. But every gesture of friendship carried an edge of doubt, as fragile as the splintered shields they fought behind.

The Sting of Betrayal

That doubt was validated one morning during a mock combat drill. Rufus was paired with Caius, a seasoned gladiator known for his cunning. The exercise was straightforward—practice offensive and defensive techniques—but Caius had his own agenda.

As Rufus lunged, Caius shifted suddenly, leaving Rufus off-balance and exposed. The movement wasn't an accident; it was a deliberate ploy to make Rufus appear inept. The lanista's harsh laugh cut through the yard.

"Rufus!" the trainer barked. "Are you trying to lose your head before you've even stepped into the arena?"

Heat rose to Rufus's face. He knew what Caius had done, and the betrayal struck a nerve. It was a minor slight, insignificant to the lanista or the other gladiators, but to Rufus, it was a reminder of the fragility of trust.

That evening, he sat apart from the group, his porridge untouched. The camaraderie he had begun to feel now seemed fragile, a mirage that could dissolve at any moment.

A Pivotal Moment

But the ludus had a way of forcing even the most guarded souls into moments of clarity.

During a sparring session the following week, Rufus faced an opponent whose sheer brute force was overwhelming. A misstep left Rufus vulnerable, his shield splintering under a heavy strike. As the next blow came down, Rufus braced for the inevitable.

But it didn't land.

Out of nowhere, Felix threw himself into the fight, deflecting the strike with his shield. The lanista's rod came down hard on Felix's back, but Felix shrugged off the punishment, his grin defiant as ever.

"Can't have the silent Dacian getting himself killed before the real fun starts," Felix said later, tossing a replacement shield at Rufus. "You owe me one."

The act of bravery left Rufus stunned. Felix had risked his safety, and for what? A quiet, guarded man who barely spoke to him? It was a revelation: trust wasn't just a risk; it was a lifeline.

Resolution: Balancing Trust and Caution

In the days that followed, Rufus began to open up, cautiously at first. He offered advice during drills, shared insights on footwork, and even allowed himself to laugh at Felix's endless stream of jokes.

Trust didn't come easily, and the fear of betrayal lingered, a shadow that refused to dissipate. But Rufus began to see that alliances were not just a survival tactic—they were a reminder of his humanity.

One evening, as the gladiators sat around the fire, Felix leaned toward Rufus, his grin as wide as ever.

"See, Silent One? You're starting to look like one of us."

"Perhaps," Rufus replied, his voice steady. "Or perhaps I'm just waiting for you to trip over your own sword."

The group erupted in laughter, and for the first time, Rufus felt a flicker of belonging. Trust was dangerous, yes. But in the unforgiving world of the ludus, isolation was far more deadly.

Rufus resolved to wield his newfound bonds wisely, knowing that while betrayal might be inevitable, the strength of brotherhood was worth the risk.

Historical Context: Brotherhood and Rivalry

In the gladiator schools of ancient Rome, relationships were forged under extraordinary circumstances. The shared struggle of training and survival created bonds that could transcend the brutality of their environment. Gladiators often relied on one another for support, both on and off the sands of the arena.

Yet, rivalries were equally common. Trainers frequently pitted gladiators against each other to assess their strengths, fostering an atmosphere of competition that made alliances both valuable and precarious. Trust was a calculated risk, but when it paid off, it often meant the difference between life and death.

Rufus's journey was not just about learning to fight—it was about learning to navigate the complexities of human connection. In the arena of life, as in the ludus, resilience isn't built in isolation. It thrives in the bonds we form, the trust we extend, and the risks we take to stand together.

Self-Help Lessons: Brotherhood in the Arena – Building Alliances

The training yard of the ludus was as much a battlefield of trust as it was of skill. Every sparring session, every shared meal, was an unspoken negotiation of loyalty and survival. Rufus had learned early on that in the arena, no one truly fought alone. Even in the direst of circumstances, alliances could mean the difference between life and death.

But alliances in the ludus were never simple. Trusting someone in a place where betrayal lurked behind every corner was like trying to balance on a blade's edge. For Rufus, whose past was steeped in loss and betrayal, the thought of relying on others felt like a gamble he wasn't sure he could afford. Yet, he soon discovered that isolation was an even greater risk.

A Lesson in Trust

The first time Felix threw Rufus a lifeline, it wasn't grand or dramatic. It was a simple gesture—half a loaf of bread offered after a particularly gruelling day of training. Rufus had been sitting alone, his muscles trembling with exhaustion, when Felix slid the bread across the table with a casual grin.

"Don't think too much of it, Dacian," Felix had said, his voice light but his eyes steady. "You'll pay me back in the arena."

It was a small act, but it planted a seed of trust. Over time, Felix became more than just a fellow gladiator. He became a mentor, a source of sharp humour and sharper advice. "The trick," Felix once told him during a sparring match, "is not just to swing harder. It's to know when to let the other guy tire himself out."

That advice applied to more than just combat. Felix had a knack for reading people, for knowing who could be trusted and who was more likely to drive a knife into your back. Under his guidance, Rufus began to navigate the intricate social dynamics of the ludus, learning how to build alliances without leaving himself vulnerable.

The Challenge of Vulnerability

But trust wasn't always rewarded. Rufus learned that the hard way when Marcus, a skilled **murmillo**, turned on him during a critical moment in training. The murmillo was a type of heavily armed gladiator, distinguished by his large rectangular shield and short sword, designed for brute force and endurance in the arena.

During a rigged drill meant to test their teamwork, Marcus exploited the exercise to outshine Rufus in front of the lanista. For Rufus, the betrayal was a harsh reminder that trust could be as dangerous as it was necessary in the unforgiving world of the ludus.

The betrayal stung deeply, not just because it left Rufus bruised and humiliated, but because it reinforced his deepest fears about relying on others. For days afterward, Rufus withdrew, his interactions with his peers reduced to curt nods and silence. It was Felix who eventually pulled him aside.

"You think the only way to survive is to keep everyone at arm's length," Felix said, his tone uncharacteristically serious. "But you'll learn, Dacian—no one gets through this alone. You just have to know who's worth the risk."

Rufus wanted to argue, but he couldn't ignore the truth in Felix's words. Isolation might protect him from betrayal, but it would also leave him without allies when he needed them most. Slowly, he began to rebuild his connections, choosing his confidants carefully and learning to balance caution with openness.

The Role of Emotional Intelligence

Building trust in the ludus required more than just observation—it required emotional intelligence. Rufus had to learn to read the subtle cues in people's behaviour: the way someone avoided eye contact when they were hiding something, or the way their tone shifted when they were being sincere. Over time, he became adept at understanding not just what people said, but what they didn't say.

In one memorable instance, Castor, a younger gladiator, confided in Rufus about his fear of the upcoming games. "I'm not ready," Castor admitted, his voice trembling. "What if I freeze out there?"

Rufus could have dismissed him or scolded him for weakness. Instead, he drew on his own experiences. "I've felt the same," Rufus said, his voice steady. "But fear isn't the enemy—it's a sign that you care about surviving. Use it. Let it sharpen your focus."

The conversation wasn't just a moment of connection; it was a turning point for Castor, who later credited Rufus's words with giving him the courage to face his first fight. For Rufus, it was a reminder that leadership wasn't about perfection—it was about authenticity and empathy.

Self-Help Lessons: The Power of Relationships in Challenging Times

Rufus's journey highlights the importance of trust, emotional intelligence, and the ability to navigate relationships in high-stakes environments. These lessons are just as relevant in our own lives, where strong connections can provide the stability and support we need to thrive.

1. Relationships as Pillars of Strength

Building trust takes time and discernment. Genuine relationships are based on mutual respect and shared goals. When nurtured, these bonds provide strength and stability during life's challenges.

2. Emotional Intelligence: A Key to Connection

Understanding your emotions and those of others is essential for building authentic connections. By recognising intentions and responding with empathy, you can navigate complex dynamics with clarity and confidence.

Practical Exercise: Building and Strengthening Your Network

1. Map Your "Support Network"

- Reflect on the people who support, inspire, and guide you.
- Write down their names and consider:
  - Who do you turn to for advice or encouragement?
  - Who challenges you to grow?
  - Who shares your values and goals?

Identify any gaps in your network. Are there relationships you need to repair or connections you'd like to cultivate?

---

2. Strengthen Relationships

Choose three people from your network and take intentional steps to deepen those connections. Examples:

- Reach out to a friend you've lost touch with and ask how they're doing.
- Express gratitude to a mentor or colleague who has guided you.
- Offer support to someone who may need it, even if they haven't asked.

Small acts of kindness and connection can have a powerful impact, strengthening bonds and building trust.

The Lesson of Brotherhood

In the unforgiving world of the ludus, Rufus discovered that true strength didn't come from isolation—it came from connection. The bonds he forged weren't perfect, but they were vital. They gave him the resilience to endure, the courage to lead, and the wisdom to navigate the challenges ahead.

In your own life, the people around you can be your greatest allies. By building trust, fostering empathy, and strengthening your connections, you can create a network of support that carries you through even the toughest battles. The arena of life is always easier to face when you're not standing alone.

Joke:

What do you call a gladiator who underestimates his opponent?

A soon-to-be-retired champion.

The Gladiator Challenge: Strength in Connection

Support Map: Reflect on your support network. Post a shout-out to someone who has supported you in your journey using #ArenaAllies.

Trust Task: Reach out to someone you haven't connected with recently. Share how it went and how they responded.

Final Reflection

Relationships, like the alliances Rufus forged, are a double-edged sword. They require effort, carry risk, and occasionally bring disappointment. But the rewards—a sense of belonging, shared strength, and mutual growth—far outweigh the risks.

Every meaningful connection you cultivate is a step toward resilience. Whether it's a friend, a mentor, or a partner, the people you trust become your allies in the arena of life. By reaching out, offering support, and expressing gratitude, you not only strengthen your bonds but also remind yourself of the value of connection.

Chapter 5:

The First Fight – Facing Fear

The Roar of the Crowd

The noise hit Rufus like a thunderclap. It wasn't just sound—it was alive, a writhing beast of cheers, jeers, and stomping feet that reverberated through the stone walls of the holding area. Above the din, the rhythmic pounding of drums added an almost primal cadence to the anticipation of violence.

Rufus stood motionless, his hands gripping the worn leather straps of his shield and sword. The coarse linen of his tunic clung to his back, damp with sweat that wasn't just from the heat. His heart hammered against his ribs, and his breathing was shallow, ragged.

Next to him, Felix leaned casually against the wall, as though waiting for nothing more than a casual stroll in the market. He turned to Rufus with a grin. "Breathe, Silent One. If you faint before the fight, it'll be the shortest career in arena history."

Rufus tried to force a smile, but his mouth was too dry.

The Walk to the Arena

The gates ahead groaned as they creaked open, spilling sunlight into the corridor. The gladiators shuffled forward, one by one, their footsteps heavy with resolve or resignation. Rufus moved with them, his legs stiff and uncooperative.

"Keep your shield up," Felix whispered as they reached the edge of the arena. "And for Jupiter's sake, don't trip. The sand's slippery when you're sweating fear."

The words, though meant to tease, settled something in Rufus. He nodded silently, focusing on his breathing.

As he stepped out into the blinding sunlight, the noise of the crowd surged to a deafening roar. Rufus blinked against the glare, his eyes adjusting to the vast expanse of the arena. The sand stretched out before him, golden and treacherous, dotted with the marks of previous fights. High above, the crowd loomed—a sea of faces, some eager, some indifferent, all hungry for blood.

Rufus raised his sword in a hesitant salute, as he'd been instructed, before stepping into position.

Facing the Enemy

His opponent was already waiting. A hulking man with arms like tree trunks and a sword that gleamed menacingly in the sun. His face was expressionless, his eyes cold and unyielding. Every movement was deliberate, every step calculated.

Rufus's stomach churned. He forced himself to recall the lanista's training: *Watch his movements. Anticipate his strikes. Stay balanced.*

The trumpet blared, and the fight began.

The first strike came fast, a blur of steel aimed at Rufus's midsection. He raised his shield just in time, the impact reverberating through his arm. His opponent pressed forward with relentless aggression, each swing of the sword more powerful than the last.

Rufus stumbled backward, his feet struggling for purchase in the loose sand. The crowd roared its approval at the display of dominance, but their noise was little more than a muffled hum beneath the pounding of Rufus's heartbeat.

The Sting of Fear

Fear was a living thing, coiled tight in Rufus's chest, its claws raking at his thoughts. He could feel its weight, its suffocating grip that threatened to paralyse him.

The lanista's voice echoed in his mind: *"The arena doesn't reward hesitation. It punishes it."*

Rufus blocked another strike, his shield trembling under the force. But his arms were tiring, and his legs felt like lead. He slipped in the sand, landing hard on one knee. His opponent seized the moment, raising his sword for a final, devastating blow.

Turning the Tide

Instinct took over. Rolling to the side, Rufus narrowly avoided the strike. The blade bit into the sand where his head had been moments before. Adrenaline surged through him, sharpening his focus.

As Rufus scrambled to his feet, he locked eyes with his opponent, whose smug expression barely shifted.

"You've got some fight in you after all," the man growled, circling slowly. "Too bad it's as clumsy as your footwork."

Rufus smirked, despite the sweat streaming down his face. "Not as clumsy as swinging at thin air," he shot back, flicking his eyes toward the shallow groove in the sand.

The man's lip curled. "Keep talking, Dacian. Maybe they'll applaud your jokes when you're flat on your back."

Rufus shrugged, his grip on the sword tightening. "They seem to like me standing just fine."

The banter seemed to fuel the crowd, their cheers rising with every exchange. Rufus shifted his stance, his confidence growing as he saw the faint flicker of annoyance cross his opponent's face.

When the next blow came, Rufus was ready. He sidestepped with deliberate precision, his sword slicing through the air to graze his opponent's arm. It wasn't deep, but it drew blood—and, judging by the man's startled grimace, it stung both body and pride.

The crowd roared, a ripple of surprise and excitement surging through the arena.

"You'll pay for that, runt," the man snarled, adjusting his grip on his weapon.

Rufus tilted his head, the smirk returning. "I thought you were the one getting paid. Or did I cut your allowance, too?"

Victory in the Sand

With renewed determination, Rufus pressed the advantage. He deflected his opponent's strikes with precision, his movements guided by the endless drills he had endured in the ludus. Finally, he saw his chance—a momentary lapse in the man's defence.

Rufus lunged, his sword striking with all the strength he could muster. The blow wasn't fatal, but it was enough to disarm his opponent and send him sprawling into the sand.

The arena erupted in applause, the crowd's excitement a tidal wave that crashed over Rufus. He stood there, chest heaving, his sword still raised, as the referee signalled the end of the fight.

A Bittersweet Victory

As the cheers echoed around him, Rufus felt an unexpected hollowness. The victory was his, but the price of it lingered in the back of his mind. His opponent was led away, bloodied and defeated, and Rufus couldn't help but wonder how close he had come to being the one dragged from the sand.

He raised his sword in salute, as tradition demanded, but his heart wasn't in it. The fight had been a test of his strength and courage, but it had also revealed the depths of his fear.

Back in the holding area, Felix greeted him with a slap on the back and a grin. "Not bad for your first time, Silent One. Next time, maybe try to win without looking like a deer caught in torchlight."

Rufus managed a faint smile, the weight of the experience still pressing down on him. "Next time," he murmured, his voice steady but quiet.

The fight was over, but the lessons it had taught him—about fear, resilience, and the thin line between life and death—would stay with him. The arena had demanded his courage, and though he had survived, Rufus knew his battles were far from over.

Historical Context: Gladiators and the Arena

In ancient Rome, the arena was more than a battleground—it was a stage where life and death played out for the entertainment of thousands. Gladiators were expected to salute the emperor and crowd before combat, a gesture of respect and submission.

Success in the arena often hinged on a gladiator's ability to stay calm under pressure. Panic could be fatal, while composure allowed for strategic thinking and adaptability. Training emphasised these qualities, preparing gladiators to face a variety of opponents and scenarios.

The First Step on a Long Journey

Rufus's first fight was both a trial and a triumph. It forced him to confront his fears, rely on his training, and find strength in the face of overwhelming odds. The victory, though bittersweet, ignited a spark of confidence—a reminder that even in the most unforgiving arenas, survival was possible.

The road ahead was uncertain, but Rufus was no longer the same man who had stumbled into the ludus months ago. He had faced the sands, battled his doubts, and emerged stronger. And though the arena's challenges were far from over, he was ready to face them, one fight at a time.

Self-Help Lessons: The First Fight – Facing Fear

The sunlight poured into the arena as the gates creaked open, illuminating the vast expanse of sand. Rufus stood at the threshold, his chest rising and falling in quick, shallow breaths. Beyond the gates, the crowd erupted into a deafening roar, their voices a chaotic mix of excitement, bloodlust, and expectation. His fingers tightened around the hilt of his gladius, the leather-wrapped grip slick with sweat.

This was it—his first fight. No amount of training in the ludus had truly prepared him for this moment. The stakes were real now, the opponent deadly, and failure meant more than bruised pride. It meant death.

Facing Fear

Rufus's heart raced as he stepped onto the sand, each grain shifting beneath his feet. His opponent, a towering **murmillo**, stood on the opposite side, his gladius glinting in the harsh sunlight. The murmillo, a heavily armed gladiator trained for endurance and brute force, carried a massive rectangular shield and a short sword. His sheer presence was intimidating, his arms like tree trunks, his armour catching the light like a warning.

The murmillo raised his shield in a mock salute, a smirk playing on his lips. To him, Rufus was just another newcomer—a lamb sent to the slaughter.

Fear coursed through Rufus, tightening his chest and clouding his thoughts. It wasn't the first time he'd felt fear, but this was different. This was primal, a raw instinct screaming at him to run. He knew, though, that there was no escape. The only way out was through.

He took a deep breath, steadying his trembling hands. The lanista's words echoed in his mind: *"Fear is natural, but don't let it control you. Use it. Let it sharpen your focus."* Rufus exhaled slowly, grounding himself. The crowd's roar faded into the background, and for a moment, it was just him and his opponent.

Turning Fear into Action

The murmillo charged, his footsteps thundering across the arena. Rufus raised his shield, bracing for impact. The murmillo's sword struck with the force of a battering ram, reverberating through Rufus's arm. Pain shot up his shoulder, but he held firm, sidestepping to deflect the next blow.

Fear didn't disappear—it was still there, gnawing at the edges of his mind. But Rufus realized he could use it. Fear heightened his senses, made him more alert. He noticed the murmillo's patterns: the way his shoulders tensed before a swing, the slight pause as he adjusted his stance.

Rufus moved with purpose, each step calculated. When the murmillo lunged again, Rufus ducked, pivoting to deliver a quick strike to his opponent's side. It wasn't enough to wound him, but it threw the murmillo off balance, forcing him to retreat. The crowd erupted in cheers, their allegiance shifting as they recognised Rufus's tenacity.

The Role of Preparation

The hours of gruelling drills in the ludus came flooding back. He remembered the repetitive strikes, the endless footwork exercises, and the relentless corrections from the trainers. At the time, it had felt like punishment. Now, he understood their purpose.

Each movement felt instinctive, guided by muscle memory. The murmillo swung high, and Rufus ducked low, his shield angled perfectly to deflect the blow. The murmillo charged, and Rufus sidestepped, his gladius grazing the man's armour.

The murmillo's frustration grew evident. He was used to overwhelming his opponents with brute strength, but Rufus's agility and precision were wearing him down. The fight turned into a battle of endurance, each man testing the other's limits.

The Final Blow

In a moment of clarity, Rufus saw his opening. The murmillo overextended, his shield dropping just slightly. Rufus seized the opportunity, stepping forward and delivering a decisive strike to the murmillo's thigh. The man fell to one knee, his sword slipping from his grasp.

The arena fell silent, the crowd holding its breath. Rufus stood over his opponent, his gladius raised. He could end it now, claim his victory in blood. But as he looked into the murmillo's eyes, he saw the humanity beneath the armour—the same fear, the same struggle for survival.

Rufus lowered his gladius, stepping back. The referee declared him the winner, and the crowd erupted into thunderous applause. For Rufus, the victory wasn't just in surviving—it was in choosing integrity over cruelty, in proving to himself that fear didn't define him.

Self-Help Lessons: Turning Fear into Strength

Rufus's first fight is a testament to the power of managing fear. Life may not place us in arenas with swords and shields, but fear is a constant companion in our own battles—whether it's a daunting presentation, a difficult conversation, or a major life change. Here's how to harness fear and turn it into strength.

1. Fear is Natural: Courage is Acting in Spite of It

Fear is a signal that you're stepping out of your comfort zone, where growth happens. Like Rufus, acknowledge your fear without letting it paralyse you. Take one step forward, then another. Each action builds courage.

---

2. Preparation is Key: Confidence Comes from Readiness

Preparation doesn't eliminate fear, but it gives you the tools to face it. Whether it's practising a speech, rehearsing a difficult conversation, or training for a new skill, preparation builds confidence and ensures you're ready when the moment comes.

Practical Exercise: Preparing for Your Own Fight

1. Visualise a Challenging Situation

- Close your eyes and imagine yourself in a scenario that intimidates you.
- Picture the sights, sounds, and feelings. Let the fear surface, then visualise yourself handling the situation successfully.

---

2. Create a Battle Plan

- Identify a specific fear or challenge.
- Break it down into manageable steps.
  - Example: For public speaking, start by practising in front of a mirror, then a small group, then a larger audience.
- Write down your plan and take the first step.

---

3. Build a Confidence Ritual

- Before facing a challenge, create a ritual to calm your mind and focus your energy:
  - Take three deep breaths.
  - Use positive self-talk, such as, *"I've prepared for this. I can handle it."*
  - Visualise a successful outcome.

The Takeaway

Fear is not a weakness—it's an invitation to grow. Like Rufus, you have the ability to face your challenges, one step at a time. With preparation, focus, and the courage to act, you can turn fear into strength and emerge victorious in the arenas of your own life.

Joke:

Why did the gladiator laugh at his opponent's insults?

Because he knew sticks and stones couldn't hurt him—only swords could.

The Gladiator Challenge: Face the Unknown

Visualisation Task: Identify a fear you want to overcome. Write a post about how you'll tackle it and share a motivational quote or mantra that resonates with you using #FaceYourFear #GladiatorChallenge.

Action Task: Take one step to confront this fear and document the process. It could be a video, photo, or written post.

Final Reflection

Fear is inevitable, but it doesn't have to define you. Every time you act in spite of fear, you build courage. Every step you take to prepare, you build confidence. Like Rufus in his first fight, you may not feel ready when the moment comes, but your readiness and determination will carry you through.

Facing fear is not about erasing it—it's about proving to yourself that you are stronger than the doubts that try to hold you back. With each challenge you overcome, you forge resilience, sharpen your skills, and take another step toward becoming the gladiator of your own life.

The arena awaits. Will you step forward?

Chapter 6:

Adapting to the Arena – Flexibility and Strategy

The arena was an unrelenting teacher. Its lessons were harsh, its stakes high, and its outcomes unforgiving. For Rufus, it wasn't enough to swing a sword or raise a shield—he needed to think, to anticipate, to outmanoeuvre opponents who were as desperate to survive as he was. The arena wasn't just a battleground; it was a living chessboard, each fight demanding more than brute strength. Victory required strategy, flexibility, and a deep understanding of the game being played.

The Lesson of Adaptability

Rufus's first test came in the form of Marcus, a murmillo whose bulk and skill made him a formidable opponent. Marcus was a seasoned fighter, his movements fluid despite his heavy armour. His large, rectangular shield was an impenetrable barrier, and his gladius struck with the precision of a viper.

As the sparring match began, Marcus advanced with relentless force. His strikes were deliberate, each one aimed to unbalance Rufus and exploit his inexperience. Rufus struggled to parry the blows, his shield vibrating under the sheer power of Marcus's attacks. Sand flew around them, kicked up by their shifting feet, as Rufus retreated step by step.

"Is that all you've got, Dacian?" Marcus taunted, his voice calm, almost bored. "I've seen laundry blow harder than your sword arm."

Rufus gritted his teeth, shooting back between gasps, "At least I'm not built like the laundry press."

From the sidelines, the lanista shouted, "Think, Rufus! A sword is only as good as the brain behind it!"

Rufus grimaced, his breath coming in short gasps. His arms burned, and his grip on the hilt of his sword faltered. Then his eyes caught something—the uneven patches of sand beneath their feet, churned up from earlier bouts. An idea began to form.

The next time Marcus charged, Rufus sidestepped rather than blocking. He manoeuvred the murmillo toward the patch of disturbed sand. As Marcus shifted his weight to strike again, his footing wavered just enough to break his rhythm.

"Careful, Marcus!" Rufus called with mock concern. "Wouldn't want you falling flat in front of an audience!"

Marcus snarled, his balance faltering. Rufus seized the moment, lunging forward with a rapid series of strikes that forced Marcus onto the defensive.

The lanista clapped his hands, a rare sign of approval. "Now you're learning," he said, though his expression hinted he wouldn't tolerate much more banter.

Understanding the Roles

Rufus realized that his battles wouldn't always be against a murmillo like Marcus. The arena was a theatre of contrasts, each gladiator trained for a specific style of combat. To survive, Rufus needed to know not just his own strengths but also the roles of his adversaries.

The **retiarius**, armed with a trident and net, was quick and elusive. Their strategy relied on ensnaring opponents and delivering precise strikes, their light armour allowing them to outpace heavier foes.

The **murmillo**, like Marcus, was a tank—slow but nearly unstoppable, relying on raw strength and defensive mastery to dominate.

The **Thracian**, with a curved **sica**—a short, sharp sword designed for slicing rather than stabbing—and a small, lightweight shield, was all about agility. Their fighting style involved darting in and out of range, aiming for weak points in an opponent's defence and wearing them down over time with precise, calculated strikes. The sica's unique shape allowed the Thracian to target areas that were harder to reach with a straight blade, adding a layer of strategy to their movements.

Each role had its strengths and vulnerabilities, and Rufus began to study them obsessively. Against a murmillo, he would use speed and precision. Against a retiarius, he would maintain a strong defensive stance, waiting for the net to miss its mark. Against a Thracian, he would focus on endurance, conserving energy until an opportunity presented itself.

Using the Arena Itself

The arena was more than a battleground—it was a weapon. Its shifting sands, uneven patches, and defined boundaries could be turned to an advantage or a downfall. Rufus learned that terrain was as much an opponent as the man in front of him.

In one match, Rufus faced a Thracian whose speed was overwhelming. The gladiator danced around him, delivering quick, stinging blows that left Rufus bruised and frustrated. The crowd loved it, their cheers feeding the Thracian's confidence.

Desperation pushed Rufus to scan his surroundings. That's when he spotted it: a patch of sand darker and heavier than the rest, dampened by spilled water. An idea sparked.

Feigning retreat, Rufus backed toward the patch, his shield raised defensively. The Thracian, emboldened, followed, closing the distance. As soon as the gladiator stepped onto the wet sand, his movements slowed, his agility hampered. Rufus didn't hesitate. He pivoted sharply, slamming his shield into the Thracian's chest and following with a powerful strike that sent the man sprawling.

The crowd roared with approval, their cheers echoing off the arena walls. Rufus stood tall, his chest heaving, and for the first time, he allowed himself to feel pride—not just in his victory, but in the strategy that had made it possible.

The Mentor's Role

Back in the training yard, the lanista approached Rufus with a rare smirk. "Not bad, Dacian," he said, clapping Rufus on the shoulder. "But don't let it go to your head. One clever trick won't save you every time."

Felix, watching from nearby, added with a grin, "He's right, you know. Next time, try not to make it look so easy—you're making the rest of us look bad."

Rufus chuckled despite himself, the tension of the day easing in the warmth of camaraderie. But he knew Felix and the lanista were both right. The arena would only grow more dangerous, and his adaptability would be tested again and again.

That night, as he lay on his pallet under the stars, Rufus replayed the day's events in his mind. For the first time, he felt not just the weight of survival but the thrill of possibility. He was learning, growing. And with each battle, he was becoming not just a fighter, but a gladiator in every sense of the word.

Self-Help Lessons: Adapting to the Arena – Flexibility and Strategy

The arena was never the same twice. Each fight brought new challenges: an unfamiliar opponent, a sudden change in weather, or the subtle shifts in the sand beneath Rufus's feet. These weren't just obstacles—they were tests of his ability to adapt. For Rufus, survival depended not on brute force alone but on the ability to read his surroundings, anticipate the unexpected, and adjust his tactics in the heat of battle.

Learning the Art of Adaptability

The fight began as it always did, with the sound of the trumpet echoing across the arena. Rufus squared off against a retiarius—a gladiator armed with a trident and net. Unlike the heavily armoured murmillos Rufus had fought before, this opponent was quick and agile, darting around the arena with unnerving speed.

The retiarius's first attack came in a blur, the net snapping toward Rufus's legs. Instinctively, Rufus leapt back, narrowly avoiding the trap. The crowd roared its approval, thrilled by the close call. Rufus's pulse quickened, but he didn't let the fear take over. He steadied himself, observing the retiarius's movements.

The retiarius relied on his speed, using the open terrain to his advantage. If Rufus tried to chase him down, he'd tire himself out before he could land a blow. He needed a new approach—something that would turn the retiarius's agility against him.

Turning the Tide

Rufus noticed that the retiarius had a pattern: he darted left after each failed net throw, resetting his stance for another attempt. Rufus decided to use this predictability to his advantage. Feigning a stumble, he lured the retiarius closer. When the net came flying again, Rufus sidestepped, allowing it to skim harmlessly past him.

With his opponent off balance, Rufus lunged forward, driving the edge of his shield into the retiarius's shoulder. The smaller man staggered, and for the first time, Rufus had the upper hand. Rufus used his superior strength and control to crowd his opponent, closing the distance and limiting the retiarius's ability to reposition or reset his attacks. Staying within striking range, Rufus delivered a clean, decisive blow, earning a thunderous cheer from the crowd.

The Lesson: Flexibility Wins the Day

Walking back to the holding area, Rufus reflected on the fight. He hadn't won because he was stronger or faster. He had won because he adapted. The retiarius had been a challenge unlike any he'd faced before, but by staying calm, observing, and adjusting his tactics, Rufus turned a disadvantage into an opportunity.

Self-Help Lessons: Adapting in Life's Arena

Rufus's fight with the retiarius is a powerful metaphor for the unpredictability of life. Challenges often come at us from unexpected angles, and rigid plans can crumble in the face of sudden changes. Adaptability is the skill that allows us to navigate these moments with grace and resilience.

---

1. Adaptability is Essential in Unpredictable Situations

Life's challenges rarely come with a warning. Job loss, relationship conflicts, or sudden health issues can throw us off course. Like Rufus, we must learn to pivot quickly and embrace flexibility, finding new paths to our goals when old ones are blocked. Adaptability isn't about giving up—it's about finding a way forward, no matter the circumstances.

---

2. Pause, Assess, and Strategise

When faced with an unexpected challenge, take a moment to pause and evaluate. Acting on impulse often leads to mistakes, but a deliberate assessment can reveal opportunities you might have missed. Ask yourself:

- What resources do I have?
- What are my strengths in this situation?
- What is the best next step to take?

By pausing and planning, you position yourself to act with purpose rather than panic.

Practical Exercise: Sharpening Your Adaptability

These exercises will help you build the mental flexibility needed to handle life's inevitable surprises.

---

1. Reflect on a Recent Setback

Think about a time when something didn't go as planned:

- What was the situation?
- How did you initially respond?
- What emotions did you experience?
- In hindsight, could you have approached it differently?

By analysing past setbacks, you can identify patterns in your reactions and develop strategies for similar challenges in the future.

---

2. Create a "Plan B" Worksheet

For any current goal or project, imagine what could go wrong and prepare a backup plan:

- **Primary Goal:** What are you aiming for?
- **Potential Obstacles:** What challenges might arise?
- **Alternative Actions:** What's your "plan B" if things don't go as expected?

Example:

- **Primary Goal:** Complete a major work project by the deadline.
- **Obstacle:** Sudden changes in priorities or team dynamics.
- **Plan B:** Prioritise the most critical tasks, delegate less urgent ones, and communicate openly with your team.

---

3. Practise "What If" Scenarios

Choose a real or hypothetical situation and brainstorm three alternative ways to handle it. For example:

- **Scenario:** You lose your job unexpectedly.
- **Option 1:** Reach out to your network for leads.

- **Option 2:** Upskill through online courses to broaden your opportunities.
- **Option 3:** Take on temporary freelance work to stay afloat while searching for a long-term role.

This exercise helps you think creatively and prepares you to respond effectively when life throws you a curveball.

The Takeaway

Life, like the arena, is unpredictable. Success doesn't always go to the strongest or the fastest—it goes to those who can adapt. By embracing flexibility, pausing to assess challenges, and preparing for contingencies, you can navigate even the most unexpected situations with confidence.

The sands of your own arena are always shifting, but with the right mindset and strategies, you can find your footing and thrive. Adaptability isn't just a skill—it's a way of turning challenges into opportunities and setbacks into stepping stones. The next time life demands a pivot, remember Rufus's lesson: stay calm, stay observant, and stay flexible.

Joke:

Why don't gladiators fear the arena?

Because every fight has the potential for a standing ovation.

The Gladiator Challenge: Pivot and Adapt

Plan B Worksheet: Post about a recent setback and share two alternative approaches you could take. Use #AdaptLikeAGladiator.

Reflection Task: Share a moment when flexibility helped you overcome a challenge. What did you learn from adapting?

Final Reflection

Adaptability isn't about avoiding challenges—it's about thriving in their presence. Every setback, every unexpected turn, is an opportunity to reassess, strategise, and grow. Like Rufus, who turned the uncertainties of the arena into opportunities for victory, you too can turn life's unpredictability into a source of strength.

The next time the ground shifts beneath your feet, don't fear it—use it. The arena is yours to conquer. How will you adapt?

Chapter 7:

The Turning Point – Building Inner Strength

The ludus was as unforgiving as ever, yet something had shifted for Rufus. He was no longer the silent outsider or the unsure novice struggling to find his footing. Now, when the younger recruits stumbled or froze during training, they turned their eyes to him. And Rufus, despite his own insecurities, found himself stepping into the role of a mentor.

Emerging Leadership

It wasn't a role Rufus sought, and certainly not one he welcomed at first. Leadership came quietly, without announcement or grand gesture. At first, it was just the subtle way the recruits mimicked his movements during drills or lingered nearby when the trainers barked for everyone to disperse. Rufus didn't notice until one evening, when a young gladiator named Livius approached him with wide, uncertain eyes.

"Rufus," Livius began, clutching his practice sword awkwardly. "How do you stay steady when... when they're watching?" He gestured toward the shadow of the arena looming beyond the training yard.

For a moment, Rufus hesitated, unsure of what to say. He wanted to brush the boy off, to claim he had no answers, but something stopped him. He saw in Livius's face a reflection of himself—a younger, rawer version of the man he'd been when he first arrived.

"You don't block out the crowd," Rufus said slowly, his voice quiet but firm. "You let them push you forward. Their noise... it's energy. Turn it into fuel. Trust your training. Trust yourself."

Livius nodded, though his nervous grip on the sword didn't loosen. Rufus sighed, a flicker of understanding lighting within him. The recruits didn't just need technique; they needed guidance. And perhaps, so did he.

Internal Conflict

The weight of responsibility crept in gradually, settling like a leaden cloak over Rufus's shoulders. The more the recruits looked to him, the heavier it became. Each question, each glance, was a reminder that his words and actions mattered—not just to him, but to the men who saw him as a leader.

Late at night, after the rest of the ludus had fallen silent, Rufus sat by the dim light of a torch, tracing the scars that crisscrossed his arms. Each one told a story: the reckless blow that had left him exposed in a sparring match, the strike he hadn't dodged in time during his first fight, the wound that had nearly cost him his life.

He muttered to himself, shaking his head. "Rufus the Leader," he said dryly, the words heavy with irony. "Next, they'll be asking me how to bake bread or charm the lanista."

The thought of Castor, the wiry recruit who had challenged him days ago, returned unbidden.

"What do you know of leading us?" Castor had spat, his voice trembling with anger and fear. "You act like you're better than us, but you're just as scared. You just hide it better."

The words had struck like a blade. Rufus had stood silent, letting them hang in the air. He couldn't deny them. Fear was a constant companion, one he carried into every fight, every decision.

Now, alone by the torchlight, Rufus allowed a wry smile to creep onto his face. "He's not wrong," he said quietly, glancing at a particularly nasty scar on his forearm. "But if he thinks he can hide better than I can, he's welcome to try wearing this face during training."

He leaned back, his smile fading into a pensive frown. The doubts still gnawed at him, but he couldn't shake Felix's teasing words from earlier that day: *"You're practically a philosopher now, Rufus. All you're missing is the toga and some grapes."*

Rufus smirked to himself. Maybe being a leader wasn't about being fearless. Maybe it was just about pretending well enough to fool everyone—including yourself.

The Turning Point

The answer came during a mock battle the next day. Livius was paired with a larger, more aggressive opponent. The trainers barked orders, but it was clear Livius was faltering. His movements were hesitant, his blocks clumsy.

When the opponent pressed forward, Livius froze entirely. The trainers shouted at him to move, their harsh voices cutting through the air, but Livius stood rooted, his sword dangling uselessly by his side.

The scene was painfully familiar to Rufus. He had been Livius once, paralysed by fear, drowning in the weight of his own insecurities. Without hesitation, Rufus stepped into the circle, his hand resting firmly on Livius's shoulder.

"Look at me," Rufus said, his tone steady and calm. "I know what it feels like. I've been where you are—frozen, unsure, terrified. But listen to me: fear doesn't make you weak. Standing here, facing it, does."

The boy's breathing slowed, his grip on the sword tightening. Rufus gave a nod of encouragement. "Trust yourself. You've got this."

When the fight resumed, Livius was still clumsy, but he didn't freeze again. He finished the match standing, and though his strikes lacked finesse, he walked away with his head held higher than before.

Watching from the edge of the yard, Felix smirked. "You've got a knack for this, Rufus. Maybe the lanista should start paying you extra."

Rufus snorted, shaking his head, but Felix's words stayed with him. Perhaps leadership wasn't about being fearless or perfect.

Perhaps it was about standing firm, even when you were riddled with doubts, and sharing that strength with others.

Redefining Leadership

In the days that followed, Rufus embraced his new role with quiet determination. He began offering more than just technique—he shared the lessons he'd learned through his own struggles, the ones that left scars but also made him stronger.

"Your shield isn't just to block blows," he told one recruit during a sparring session. "It's part of your offence. Use it to create space, to unbalance your opponent. Every tool has more than one use—just like every fighter has more than one strength."

At night, as he lay on his pallet, Rufus no longer felt the gnawing weight of his doubts. The burden of leadership was still there, but it had shifted. It wasn't something to fear or avoid—it was something to rise to, just as he'd risen to every challenge in the arena.

For the first time, Rufus began to see himself not just as a survivor but as a guide, someone who could help others navigate the same treacherous path he had walked. And in doing so, he found a strength he hadn't known he possessed.

The scars on his body, once a reminder of his failures, now felt like badges of resilience. They were proof that he had endured—and that he could lead others to do the same.

Historical Context: Leadership in the Ludus

In the gladiator schools of ancient Rome, leadership was not bestowed through titles but earned through respect. Seasoned gladiators often took on the role of mentors, teaching recruits the skills and strategies that could mean the difference between life and death.

Scars, far from being seen as weaknesses, were symbols of resilience. They told stories of survival, of battles fought and endured. Gladiators who bore their scars with pride often inspired their peers, proving that even in the face of unimaginable hardship, one could endure and rise again.

Rising Above the Chains

Rufus's journey toward leadership was not a smooth ascent. It was marked by doubt, failure, and moments of vulnerability. But it was these very struggles that shaped him into a mentor worth following. He realized that his scars, far from disqualifying him, were the very proof of his strength.

As he stood in the training yard, watching the recruits spar under his guidance, Rufus felt a quiet sense of purpose. He wasn't just surviving the ludus—he was helping others survive too. And in doing so, he found a strength he hadn't known he possessed: the strength to rise above his chains, not by standing alone, but by lifting others with him.

The arena awaited them all. Together, they would face it.

Self-Help Lessons: The Turning Point – Building Inner Strength

The yard of the ludus was quieter than usual, the clang of swords replaced by the low murmur of recruits grappling with their own fears. Rufus stood at the edge of the training ground, watching a young gladiator named Castor struggle to lift his shield. The boy's frame trembled under its weight, his face a mask of frustration and despair. Rufus remembered that feeling all too well—the crushing sense of inadequacy, the haunting question: *Am I strong enough?*

Rufus's journey to this moment had been anything but smooth. His scars, both physical and emotional, were a map of the battles he had fought—not all of them won. Yet, as he watched Castor falter, Rufus realized something: his scars were also a map of lessons learned, each one a story of resilience and growth. The very struggles that had once made him feel weak now gave him the strength to guide others.

From Survivor to Mentor

Rufus approached Castor, his shadow falling over the boy. "It doesn't get lighter," he said, his voice steady but kind. "You just get stronger."

Castor looked up, doubt clouding his eyes. "And if I'm not strong enough?"

Rufus crouched beside him, gripping the edge of the shield. "You will be. But strength isn't just in your arms. It's in your will to keep lifting, even when you think you can't."

It wasn't a grand speech, but it didn't need to be. Rufus knew that words alone wouldn't transform the boy—it was the effort that would. As Castor nodded and adjusted his grip, Rufus stayed by his side, offering corrections and encouragement. The boy's progress was slow, but it was progress, and that was enough.

In that moment, Rufus realized the truth about leadership: it wasn't about being perfect or invincible. It was about showing up, sharing your experience, and believing in others until they could believe in themselves.

Finding Purpose in Service

Leadership didn't come naturally to Rufus. For a long time, he saw himself as a lone survivor, focused solely on his own battles. But over time, the recruits started looking to him—not because he was the strongest, but because he understood their struggles. He had walked their path, stumbled over the same obstacles, and found a way forward.

One evening, Felix, the veteran gladiator who had once guided Rufus, approached him with a grin. "You've become the one they watch, you know."

Rufus frowned. "What do you mean?"

Felix gestured toward the younger recruits gathered in the yard. "They follow your lead. When you fight, they watch to learn. When you speak, they listen. You're more than just a gladiator now—you're their anchor."

The words unsettled Rufus at first. He didn't feel like a leader. He still had doubts, still struggled with the weight of his own fears. But as he continued to guide the younger gladiators, something shifted. The act of helping others gave him a sense of purpose that transcended his personal struggles. It wasn't about being perfect—it was about being present.

Real-World Leadership Lessons

Rufus's story mirrors countless real-world examples of leadership born from adversity. Consider Nelson Mandela, who emerged from 27 years of imprisonment not with bitterness, but with a commitment to reconciliation and unity. His scars became symbols of resilience, his struggles a foundation for guiding others toward hope and progress.

Leadership doesn't demand that we have all the answers. It asks us to share what we've learned, to stand by others in their struggles, and to inspire them to find their own strength. Whether it's mentoring a colleague, supporting a friend, or leading a team through uncertainty, true leadership is about service, not self.

Self-Help Lessons: Strength in Leadership and Service

Rufus's journey from a hesitant mentor to a respected leader teaches us that leadership is less about commanding and more about empowering. It's about turning your scars into lessons and using your experiences to uplift others.

---

1. From Survivor to Leader

Your struggles don't disqualify you from leading—they equip you for it. The challenges you've faced give you empathy and insight, making you uniquely qualified to guide others. Leadership isn't about having all the answers; it's about sharing the journey and saying, "You're not alone."

---

2. Strength in Service

Serving others doesn't diminish your strength—it amplifies it. When you help someone else overcome their fears or achieve their goals, you build a sense of purpose that strengthens you in return. Service is a two-way street: it uplifts the person receiving it and enriches the person giving it.

Practical Exercise: Embracing Leadership in Your Life

These exercises are designed to help you recognise your leadership potential, connect with others, and turn your scars into strengths.

---

1. Reflect on Leadership

Think about a time when you were hesitant to take on a leadership role.

- What held you back? Was it fear of failure, self-doubt, or feeling unprepared?
- How did you overcome that hesitation—or how could you have approached it differently?

Write about this experience, focusing on what it taught you about yourself and what leadership means to you.

---

2. Set Mentorship Goals

Identify one person in your life who could benefit from your guidance or support. This could be a colleague, a friend, a family member, or someone in your community.

- What specific action can you take this week to help them?

- Examples: Share advice, teach a skill, encourage them through a challenge, or simply listen.

- Set a clear goal and follow through with it.

Afterward, reflect on how the interaction impacted both you and the other person.

---

3. Embrace Your Scars

Your scars—both physical and emotional—tell the story of your resilience. Take a moment to list three challenges you've overcome in life.

- How did those experiences shape you?
- What lessons did you learn, and how can you use them to lead or mentor others?

Embrace these moments as badges of strength that have prepared you to guide others on their journeys.

The Takeaway

Leadership is not about perfection—it's about presence. It's about showing up, sharing your journey, and believing in others until they can believe in themselves. Like Rufus, you have the power to turn your struggles into strengths and your scars into symbols of resilience.

Step into your own arena of leadership with courage and authenticity. The lessons you've learned are your greatest tools for guiding others and building a legacy of strength and service.

Joke:

Why did the gladiator throw a party after blocking an attack?

Because even small victories deserve a big cheer.

The Gladiator Challenge: Lead with Purpose

Mentorship Moment: Reflect on a time when you stepped into a leadership or mentorship role, or think about a way you've been inspired by someone else's guidance. Share a general insight or lesson from that experience without naming specific individuals. Post your thoughts using **#GladiatorLeadership** to inspire others to lead with purpose.

Strength Challenge: Share one scar—physical or emotional—that represents your growth and resilience. What did it teach you?

Final Reflection

Leadership is not a destination—it's a journey. It's about rising above your fears, embracing your scars, and finding the courage to serve others despite your own uncertainties. Like Rufus, who discovered his strength in the act of lifting others, you too can uncover your potential as a leader by sharing your experiences and guiding those who need it.

Your scars are not weaknesses; they are the proof of your resilience. They show the battles you've faced and the lessons you've learned. When you use those lessons to inspire and empower others, you turn your struggles into strength—not just for yourself, but for everyone you lead.

The arena of life is full of challenges, but it's also full of opportunities to lift others. Step forward, embrace your scars, and become the leader you were always meant to be. **Your journey is not just yours—it's a torch to light the way for others.**

Chapter 8:

The Commodification of Glory

The Commodification of Glory

The training yard buzzed with an unusual energy that morning. Even the normally stoic lanista seemed more animated than usual, pacing back and forth as he barked orders at the gladiators. Rufus, catching his breath after a series of weighted drills, noticed Felix leaning against a pillar, his face split into a wide grin.

"What's got you looking like a cat that found the cream?" Rufus asked, wiping sweat from his brow.

Felix pointed to a cluster of slaves bustling near the edge of the yard, each armed with cloths and clay jars. "Haven't you heard? You're the next big sensation. The lanista's personal golden goose."

Rufus frowned, following Felix's gaze. One of the slaves approached him hesitantly, a clean linen cloth in hand.

"Master Rufus, your sweat, if you please."

"My what?" Rufus recoiled, taking a step back.

"Your sweat," Felix interjected, barely suppressing his laughter. "Apparently, the fine folk of Rome believe it's an aphrodisiac. Fetches quite the coin. You, my friend, are liquid gold."

Before Rufus could protest, the lanista's voice boomed across the yard. "Rufus! Stand still and let them do their work. This is not negotiable."

Rufus stood stiffly, his jaw clenched, as the slave dabbed his arm with a cloth and carefully wrung it into a jar. Felix leaned in with a conspiratorial grin.

"Look on the bright side," Felix said. "If this doesn't work out, maybe they'll market your tears next."

The Offer from Aurelia

That afternoon, the lanista called Rufus to his quarters, a rare occurrence that immediately set Rufus on edge. The lanista's grin was wolfish, his tone oily with satisfaction as he spoke.

"You've been summoned, Rufus," he said, reclining in his chair. "Lady Aurelia has requested your presence at her villa tonight. She's paid handsomely for the privilege."

Rufus straightened, his face unreadable. "And what does she want from me?"

The lanista's grin widened. "Her entertainment, her pleasure—your company, of course. Perhaps she wants to see if the man behind the sword is as impressive as the one on the sand."

Rufus raised an eyebrow. "If she's paying for my company, should I bring a joke book, or do you think my charm alone will suffice?"

The lanista chuckled darkly. "She's not paying for wit, Rufus. But mind you, don't forget who owns you."

The Encounter at Aurelia's Villa

As evening fell, Rufus found himself escorted to Lady Aurelia's opulent villa. He had been bathed, perfumed, and dressed in fine linen robes—nothing like the rough tunics he wore in the ludus. As he glanced down at the elegant garments, he muttered to himself, "If Felix sees me like this, I'll never hear the last of it."

Lady Aurelia greeted him in the atrium, her beauty as striking as her wealth. Draped in shimmering silk and adorned with jewels, she radiated an aura of command that reminded Rufus of the lanista, though far more refined.

"You're even more magnificent in person," she said, her voice smooth as the wine she offered him. "Come, sit. Let us enjoy the evening."

Rufus inclined his head, accepting the goblet. As he sat down, he murmured under his breath, "Enjoying the evening is exactly what Felix would call this."

Turning the Tables

As the evening progressed, Aurelia's interest deepened. She leaned closer, her touch lingering on his arm. "You've been denied so much," she murmured. "Let this night be yours as much as it is mine. Take what joy you can, Rufus. You've earned it."

Rufus, recognising the opportunity, smiled faintly. "My lady, I am honoured to be your guest. But if I may, could this evening's generosity extend to my brothers in the ludus? They have fought and bled beside me. A small feast would lift their spirits."

Aurelia laughed softly, intrigued. "You would bargain for them, rather than for yourself?"

"They're like family," he said simply. "And family has a way of reminding you of your value—especially when you least expect it."

She raised an eyebrow. "And do they tease you as well?"

"Relentlessly," Rufus replied with a smirk. "But I'll take their laughter over the lanista's any day."

A Night to Remember

The rest of the evening unfolded with an unexpected mix of charm, tension, and mischief. Lady Aurelia, clearly accustomed to commanding attention, soon discovered that Rufus was not one to be easily intimidated—even in her gilded world. The meal began as a dance of subtle flirtations and playful jabs, with Aurelia pouring wine as liberally as she poured compliments.

"You've spent so much time in the arena," she said, her voice honeyed and teasing. "It's a shame you've been denied the finer things in life. Perhaps tonight will change that."

Rufus raised his goblet, a glint of humour in his eyes. "I appreciate the sentiment, my lady. Though I must admit, the finer things usually don't come with this much fanfare—or perfume."

Aurelia laughed, her fingers trailing along the rim of her goblet. "Bold and sharp-witted. I can see why the crowds adore you. But tell me, Rufus, have you ever been overwhelmed by admiration?"

Rufus leaned back slightly, a mock-serious expression crossing his face. "Only when Felix attempts to cook. His version of stew is as deadly as any murmillo."

Aurelia arched a brow, intrigued. "Felix? A fellow gladiator, I assume?"

"My closest friend," Rufus replied, his smirk softening into something genuine. "And the loudest critic of my life decisions, no doubt including this dinner."

Aurelia chuckled, swirling her wine. "Critics often speak from jealousy, you know."

"Jealousy?" Rufus grinned. "I think Felix would sooner wrestle a lion than sit through an evening in robes like these."

The conversation flowed, interspersed with Aurelia's probing questions and Rufus's dry humour. As they moved into the villa's more intimate lounge, Aurelia's interest became bolder.

"Tell me," she said, leaning in conspiratorially, "do you gladiators share… everything? Your victories, your secrets… perhaps even your admirers?"

Rufus nearly choked on his wine but quickly composed himself. "We share many things, my lady. Though I assure you, admirers tend to prefer their affections undivided."

Aurelia laughed, delighted by his response. "Well, then," she said, her voice dipping into a sultry tone, "consider tonight an exclusive honour."

Rufus, recognising the fine line he was walking, decided to redirect the conversation with a grin. "Honoured indeed, but speaking of sharing, perhaps the wine and food could extend to my comrades? A feast might inspire some... gladiatorial poetry from Felix."

Aurelia clapped her hands, clearly entertained. "You're negotiating for your friends even now? Most men in your position would be thinking only of themselves."

Rufus shrugged, feigning innocence. "I've learned that when Felix is fed well, he complains less. It's purely self-interest."

Back at the Ludus

By the time Rufus returned to the ludus the next morning, the promised crates of fine food and wine were already being unloaded. His fellow gladiators swarmed around the bounty, their cheers echoing through the training yard.

Felix was the first to approach, clutching a loaf of bread as though it were a trophy. "Rufus, you miracle worker! I didn't think it possible, but you've managed to charm Rome's finest and bring back spoils fit for a king."

Rufus shook his head, his tone dry. "If you call bread and wine spoils, Felix, I fear for your standards."

Felix leaned in, smirking. "Oh, don't play coy, Dacian. The real question is—did you manage to keep your robe on all night?"

Rufus rolled his eyes but couldn't help the grin that tugged at his lips. "Let's just say Lady Aurelia values conversation as much as company. Not that you'd know anything about subtlety."

Felix erupted into laughter, clapping Rufus on the back. "Subtlety? That's rich coming from the man who just negotiated a feast for the entire ludus while wearing silk!"

The other gladiators joined in, their banter transforming what could have been a demeaning ordeal into a shared victory. Even the lanista, watching from a distance, seemed begrudgingly impressed.

As the men gathered to eat, Felix raised his goblet high. "To Rufus, our golden goose, who turned one night of servitude into a feast for us all. May he charm many more matrons—and bring back the wine while he's at it!"

Laughter rang out, and for a moment, the camaraderie in the ludus felt unbreakable. Rufus, seated among his comrades, allowed himself a rare moment of satisfaction. Even in a world that sought to strip him of his dignity, he had found a way to reclaim it—and to share it with those who mattered most.

Themes and Lessons

1. **Turning the Tables**

Rufus demonstrates that even in situations where he has little power, he can find ways to assert himself and advocate for others. This teaches readers the value of recognising opportunities and using them wisely.

2. **The Importance of Community**

By prioritising his comrades over his own comfort, Rufus shows that true strength lies in lifting others up. Readers can reflect on how their own actions impact the people around them.

3. **Finding Agency in Adversity**

Rufus's ability to negotiate with Aurelia highlights the importance of seeking agency, even in seemingly powerless situations. It's a reminder that even small victories can pave the way for larger ones.

Historical Insight: The Commodification of Gladiators

In ancient Rome, gladiators were both warriors and commodities. Their bodies, victories, and even their sweat were exploited for profit in a culture obsessed with power and spectacle. Roman society placed gladiators at the intersection of admiration and objectification. They were revered for their bravery and skill in the arena but simultaneously dehumanised, reduced to symbols of entertainment and merchandise.

The practice of collecting gladiatorial sweat, believed to possess aphrodisiac properties, highlights the extent to which their physicality was commodified. Wealthy Romans, particularly women, would purchase these "souvenirs" as talismans of strength or allure. Gladiators were also rented out for private entertainment, their status as enslaved combatants often leaving them powerless to refuse.

This exploitation underscores the paradox of their existence. While celebrated in public, they remained slaves, stripped of autonomy. Yet, as Rufus's story illustrates, even within such confines, gladiators could assert agency and reclaim some dignity by finding ways to influence their circumstances.

Self-Help Section: Lessons in Agency and Compassion

Rufus's encounter with Lady Aurelia offers more than just a glimpse into the strange commodification of his status—it's a masterclass in reclaiming control and using influence for good. His actions highlight timeless lessons about finding agency in adversity and the power of compassion.

1. Finding Power in Powerlessness

When faced with the lanista's orders and Aurelia's request, Rufus could have simply complied, resigned to his role as a pawn in their games. Instead, he chose to negotiate, transforming a humiliating demand into an opportunity to benefit his comrades. This act reminds us that even in situations where control feels out of reach, there are often ways to assert agency.

Reflection Questions:

- Think of a time when you felt powerless. Were there opportunities to assert control or influence the outcome?
- How can you use negotiation or creativity to shift the dynamics in challenging situations?

2. Building Strength Through Community

Rufus's decision to advocate for his fellow gladiators instead of focusing solely on himself underscores the importance of community. Strength isn't just about individual resilience—it's about lifting others up and creating collective victories.

Action Step:

- Identify one way you can support your community, workplace, or family this week. It could be as simple as sharing a resource, offering encouragement, or advocating for someone who needs help.

3. Turning Adversity into Opportunity

Rufus's ability to see Aurelia's request as a chance to help his comrades is a lesson in reframing. Instead of viewing the situation solely as exploitation, he used it to secure a tangible benefit for those around him. This teaches us to look for hidden opportunities within challenges.

Practical Exercise:

- Think of a current challenge you're facing. Write down three potential opportunities it might present—whether for personal growth, new connections, or unexpected benefits.
- Choose one actionable step to explore these opportunities further.

Joke:

Why did Rufus agree to spend the evening with Lady Aurelia?

Because if his sweat was fetching a fortune, who knew what the rest of him was worth?

The Gladiator Challenge: Finding Your Rudis of Freedom

Inspired by Rufus's story, here's your challenge:

1. **Identify an Adverse Situation:** Think of a scenario where you feel limited or powerless, whether at work, in relationships, or in personal goals.
2. **Reframe and Act:** Write down one way you can turn the situation into an opportunity. This could involve advocating for yourself or others, seeking creative solutions, or shifting your perspective.
3. **Share Your Victory:** Post about your experience on social media using #GladiatorAgency. Celebrate the small victory and inspire others to find agency in their challenges.

Rufus's ability to find power within exploitation and strength within adversity is a testament to the resilience of the human spirit. His actions remind us that, no matter how dire the circumstances, there is always room to reclaim dignity and use our influence for good. As readers, we are called to step into our own arenas, to fight not just for ourselves but for those around us, and to find opportunities even when they seem hidden in the shadows of hardship.

Chapter 9:

Betrayals and Challenges – Overcoming Setbacks

The tension in the ludus felt heavier than the armour Rufus now wore with growing confidence. Alliances in this place were as unstable as the sand beneath their feet, shifting with every whispered word and sidelong glance. Trust was a currency few dared to spend, and Rufus had learned to guard his carefully. But even he wasn't prepared for how deeply betrayal could cut.

A Betrayal Unfolds

The day started like any other, with the clang of swords and the sharp barks of the lanista echoing in the training yard. Rufus was paired with Lucius, a gladiator whose skill he respected and whose camaraderie had been a rare solace. Lucius had been there during Rufus's darkest days, offering advice and the occasional wry joke to lighten the grim reality of their lives.

Their sparring began with the usual rhythm, each man testing the other with calculated strikes and counters. But soon, Lucius's movements became sharper, his strikes more forceful. At first, Rufus assumed Lucius was pushing him to improve, a common enough practice in the ludus.

Then came the feint—a clever, deliberate shift in Lucius's stance that sent Rufus lunging forward, off-balance.

Before Rufus could recover, Lucius delivered a sweeping blow that knocked him flat into the sand. Laughter erupted from the sidelines, and when Rufus glanced toward the lanista, he saw a grin of cruel amusement.

Lucius extended a hand, and for a moment, Rufus thought it was an olive branch. "Thanks for making me look good," Lucius said under his breath, his smirk unmistakable.

Rufus took the hand, muttering through clenched teeth, "Careful, Lucius. One day, I might return the favour."

That night, Rufus sat alone, his thoughts churning. He replayed the moment over and over, anger and confusion warring within him. Trusting Lucius, he realised, had been as smart as trusting the lanista with a promise of fairness. He stared at his bruised hands and thought, *Next time, I'm aiming for his shins.*

A Rigged Fight

The betrayal might have festered longer had Rufus not been thrust into the next challenge almost immediately. The lanista summoned him with a gleeful tone that made Rufus's stomach tighten.

"Tomorrow, you'll fight in the arena," the lanista said. "It's time we see if you're worth the investment."

When Rufus stepped into the arena, the nature of the fight became clear. His opponent was a murmillo—a giant of a man clad in heavy armour, his shield broad enough to deflect any attack, his sword a gleaming instrument of death. This wasn't a fair match. It was a spectacle designed to test Rufus to the limit—or break him entirely.

The murmillo stalked forward, his every step exuding confidence. Rufus raised his lighter shield and sword, acutely aware of the disparity between them. The crowd roared, their cries a chaotic mix of anticipation and bloodlust.

The murmillo struck first, his sword slamming into Rufus's shield with such force that it sent him staggering. The crowd cheered, thrilled by the murmillo's dominance. But Rufus wasn't finished. Gritting his teeth, he used his agility to stay out of reach, circling and darting in with quick strikes to test the murmillo's defences.

A Critical Moment of Choice

The fight was a blur of movement and noise, Rufus dodging and blocking, searching for an opening. Then, out of the corner of his eye, he saw Castor—a younger gladiator who had been sent into the arena alongside him—backed against the wall of the arena, his shield splintered, his opponent bearing down on him with deadly intent.

Rufus hesitated. His instincts screamed at him to stay focused on his own fight. Turning his back on the murmillo could be a death sentence. Yet, as he watched Castor struggle, something inside him refused to look away.

With a surge of resolve, Rufus made his decision. He feinted toward the murmillo, drawing his attention for a split second, before breaking into a sprint toward Castor. Using his shield, Rufus deflected the blow aimed at Castor, the clash of steel reverberating through the arena.

The crowd gasped, then roared their approval at the unexpected act of bravery. Castor, wide-eyed and shaken, scrambled to his feet, his grip tightening on his weapon. Together, they turned the tide, their combined efforts forcing Castor's opponent into retreat.

But Rufus's gambit had left him vulnerable. The murmillo, seizing the opportunity, charged toward him with a thunderous strike. Rufus barely managed to raise his shield, the impact sending him reeling. Pain shot through his arm, but he held his ground, gritting his teeth as he faced the murmillo once more.

Resolution

The fight ended with Rufus standing battered but victorious, his chest heaving as the murmillo lay defeated at his feet. The crowd's roar was deafening, their cheers washing over him like a wave. He raised his sword in acknowledgment, but the triumph felt hollow.

Back in the holding area, Castor approached him, his expression a mix of gratitude and guilt. "You didn't have to help me," he said quietly. "But you did. I owe you my life."

Rufus shook his head. "We all face the same sands, Castor. If we don't stand together, we fall alone."

As Castor walked away, Rufus allowed himself a moment of reflection. The fight had tested more than his skill—it had tested his character, forcing him to choose between survival and integrity. Lucius's betrayal had left him questioning the value of trust, but Castor's loyalty reminded him why it mattered.

The lesson was clear: in the unforgiving world of the arena, where betrayal and danger were constants, integrity wasn't just a moral choice—it was a source of strength. And for Rufus, it was a reminder that even in the darkest moments, he could choose to rise above.

Historical Context: Corruption and Honour in the Arena

The gladiatorial games were as much a political tool as they were a form of entertainment. Matches were often manipulated to serve the interests of influential patrons or the whims of lanistas, who wielded power over their fighters. Rigged fights were not uncommon, with outcomes predetermined to curry favour or send a message.

Yet, acts of bravery and integrity had the power to transcend the corruption. The Roman crowd valued not just physical prowess but also displays of honour and morality. Gladiators who demonstrated these qualities often won the admiration of the public, elevating their status even in the face of systemic injustice.

Overcoming Setbacks with Integrity

Rufus's survival wasn't just about skill or strength—it was about choosing integrity in the face of betrayal and unfairness. His willingness to risk his own safety to save Castor proved that honour and trust could still exist in a world that often rewarded the opposite.

For Rufus, the fight was a turning point. It reinforced his belief that setbacks, no matter how unfair, could be overcome with resilience and a steadfast moral compass. His scars, both physical and emotional, were marks of survival—but more importantly, they were marks of the values he refused to compromise.

In the arena of life, as in the sands of the *ludus*, honour remains a choice. Even when the odds are stacked against you, how you face the challenge defines who you are.

Self-Help Lessons: Betrayals and Challenges – Overcoming Setbacks

The air in the ludus was thick with tension, the kind that prickled at the edges of Rufus's instincts. Betrayal wasn't an anomaly here—it was part of the environment, woven into the fabric of survival. Yet, the sting of betrayal always hit differently when it came from someone you trusted.

The Betrayal

It was Lucius, a gladiator Rufus had come to respect. Lucius, with his easy charm and quick wit, had been one of the few who seemed genuine in a world that thrived on deception. They'd fought side by side in drills, shared meals, and even exchanged stories about the lives they'd lost to the sands of the arena. But that trust crumbled during a high-stakes sparring session.

Rufus had landed a clean strike, earning a nod of approval from the lanista. But as the session neared its end, Lucius whispered under his breath, "Sorry, friend," before sweeping Rufus's legs out from under him. The move sent Rufus sprawling into the sand, his weapon clattering out of reach. The lanista laughed, and Lucius basked in the attention.

The betrayal wasn't about physical harm—it was about humiliation, about asserting dominance in front of their peers. Rufus clenched his fists, his face burning with anger and shame. Trust, once a fragile thread, had been severed.

The Moral Test

Not long after, Rufus was thrust into a rigged fight designed to stack the odds against him. His opponent, a towering murmillo favoured by the lanista, entered the arena with a confidence that bordered on arrogance. The murmillo's armour gleamed in the sunlight, a stark contrast to Rufus's battered shield and dented sword.

As the fight began, Rufus's focus narrowed to the murmillo's every movement. The murmillo's strikes were heavy and deliberate, designed to wear Rufus down rather than finish him quickly. The crowd roared with each clash of their weapons, hungry for blood and spectacle.

Out of the corner of his eye, Rufus saw Castor—young, inexperienced, and clearly outmatched by his own opponent—being driven into a corner of the arena. The murmillo took advantage of Rufus's brief distraction, slamming his shield into Rufus's chest and sending him stumbling.

A choice loomed before Rufus: stay focused on his fight or risk everything to help Castor. The logical path was clear—self-preservation. But Rufus had come to understand that survival without honour was hollow.

He made his decision in an instant. Dodging a blow from the murmillo, Rufus dashed toward Castor and intercepted a strike meant to end the boy's life. The crowd gasped as Rufus deflected the blow, giving Castor the opening he needed to recover. The murmillo, enraged by Rufus's audacity, charged with renewed fury.

The Ripple Effect

Rufus's intervention turned the tide of the fight. Castor regained his footing and joined the fray, the two of them working in tandem to outmanoeuvre the murmillo. The crowd, initially sceptical, erupted in cheers for the underdog duo. By the time the fight ended, Rufus was battered but victorious.

Back in the holding area, Castor approached him, his voice trembling with gratitude. "You didn't have to help me," he said. "But you did. I won't forget it."

Rufus nodded, his body aching but his resolve stronger than ever. He hadn't just won a fight—he had upheld his integrity, inspiring loyalty and respect in the process.

Self-Help Lessons: Building Strength Through Integrity and Resilience

Rufus's journey through betrayal and challenge teaches us that life's hardest moments often hold the greatest opportunities for growth. Integrity and resilience are not just values—they are tools for navigating adversity and building meaningful connections.

---

1. Integrity Under Pressure

True character is revealed in moments of crisis. Rufus chose to act with honour, even when it would have been easier to prioritise his survival. Similarly, in our own lives, staying true to our values—even when the stakes are high—builds strength and earns respect.

---

2. Resilience in Unfair Situations

Life is rarely fair. Like Rufus, we must focus on what we can control—our actions, our attitudes, and our ability to adapt. By channelling energy into these areas, we can turn even the most unfair situations into opportunities for growth.

---

3. The Ripple Effect of Integrity

Acts of integrity inspire trust and loyalty. When Rufus helped Castor, he not only saved the boy's life but also strengthened their bond. In your own life, leading with integrity can create a ripple effect, influencing others to act with honour and fostering stronger relationships.

Practical Exercise: Applying These Lessons to Your Life

These exercises are designed to help you navigate moral dilemmas, build resilience, and act with integrity.

---

1. Reflect on a Difficult Choice

Think back to a time when you faced a moral dilemma.

- What was the situation?
- Did you choose integrity, and why or why not?
- What were the consequences of your decision—both immediate and long-term?

Write about this experience, focusing on what it taught you about your values and character.

---

2. Learn from Setbacks

Betrayals and failures often leave scars, but they also hold valuable lessons. Reflect on a setback that deeply affected you.

- What happened?
- How did it impact you emotionally and mentally?
- Write down three lessons you learned from the experience.

Consider how these lessons have shaped your current approach to challenges and relationships.

---

3. Use a Decision-Making Matrix

When facing a moral or practical dilemma, create a decision-making matrix to evaluate your options:

1. Write down your choices.

2. List the potential short-term and long-term consequences of each choice.

3. Consider how each choice aligns with your values and goals.

This structured approach can help you make decisions that reflect your integrity and support your long-term well-being.

The Takeaway

Betrayal and unfairness are inevitable in life, but they do not have to define us. By acting with integrity and focusing on what we can control, we turn challenges into opportunities to grow stronger and forge deeper connections. Like Rufus, we all have the power to rise above adversity and inspire others through our actions.

Joke:

Why did the gladiator carry a mirror into battle?

To remind himself that the toughest opponent is the one staring back.

The Gladiator Challenge: Honour in Adversity

Moral Compass Task: Reflect on a time you made a difficult ethical decision. What guided you? Share your experience with #IntegrityInAction.

Resilience Reflection: Post about a betrayal or setback that taught you an important lesson. How did you rise above it?

Final Reflection

Setbacks, whether they come as betrayals, failures, or unfair circumstances, are inevitable. But they are not the end of the story.

How you respond to them—the choices you make, the values you uphold—defines who you are and who you become.

Rufus's journey reminds us that while we cannot control the actions of others, we can control our own. By choosing integrity, we not only build our own strength but also inspire those around us. Each act of honour, no matter how small, creates a ripple effect that can transform relationships and communities.

The arena of life will challenge you. Betrayals will test your trust. Unfairness will push you to your limits. But remember: every setback is a chance to rise again, stronger and wiser. Will you choose to stand tall, act with integrity, and inspire others in the process?

The choice is yours, and the arena is waiting.

Chapter 10:

The Final Fight – Earning Redemption

The air was thick with tension, the kind that wrapped itself around you and squeezed, making every breath feel deliberate. Rufus stood alone in the shadowed entrance to the arena, his gladius held loosely in one hand, his shield strapped tightly to the other. For all the noise above—the muffled hum of the restless crowd—this moment was quiet. Still.

He wasn't just about to face an opponent. He was about to face the culmination of every battle, every betrayal, every scar that had marked his journey. The arena had taken so much from him—his identity, his freedom—but it had also given him something he never anticipated: strength. Not the raw, reckless kind of his youth, but a tempered steel forged through failure, discipline, and resilience.

Rufus closed his eyes briefly, the faces of those who had shaped his path flashing through his mind. Felix, with his relentless humour and quiet wisdom. Castor, who had taught him the value of trust when he'd thought it impossible. Even Lucius, whose betrayal had taught Rufus the hardest lesson of all: that integrity was a choice, even when the world made it seem foolish.

The iron gate in front of him creaked open, the light of the arena flooding the dim corridor. Rufus opened his eyes, squared his shoulders, and stepped forward.

The Champion Enters

The crowd erupted into a deafening roar as Rufus emerged, their voices cascading over him like waves. But their cheers were nothing compared to the explosion that followed the opening of the opposite gate.

Draconis entered the arena like a storm. Towering, muscular, and clad in gleaming armour, the murmillo was a living legend. His shield bore the marks of countless victories, and his gladius reflected the sunlight like a divine weapon. He didn't just command the crowd's attention; he owned it.

Draconis raised his sword in a slow, deliberate salute to the stands, his confidence radiating through every movement. Then his gaze locked onto Rufus, and the smirk that spread across his face said everything: This fight wasn't a contest—it was a foregone conclusion.

The First Clash

The herald's booming voice cut through the air, silencing the crowd. "Today, we witness the might of Draconis, undefeated champion of the arena, against Rufus, the rising star of the ludus. May the gods favour the brave!"

The trumpet sounded, and Draconis moved with startling speed. His first strike was a brutal swing of his shield, meant to knock Rufus off balance. Rufus barely managed to sidestep, the rush of air from the shield's edge brushing his face.

The murmillo didn't pause. He followed with a downward slash, forcing Rufus to raise his own shield to deflect it. The impact reverberated through his arm, sending a sharp jolt of pain to his shoulder.

Rufus gritted his teeth and retreated a few steps, studying Draconis's movements. The champion was powerful, yes, but his attacks were designed to overwhelm. They were almost... predictable.

Fighting Smart

Rufus began to move, circling Draconis, using the terrain to his advantage. He noticed the subtle shifts in the sand, the way certain areas were firmer while others gave way underfoot. Draconis, confident in his brute strength, didn't seem to pay attention to such details.

The murmillo charged again, his gladius cutting through the air. Rufus ducked low, letting the blade pass overhead, then pivoted sharply to strike at Draconis's side. His gladius found its mark, glancing off the armour but causing the murmillo to stagger.

The crowd gasped, their allegiance starting to waver. Rufus pressed the advantage, using his agility to stay just out of reach of Draconis's crushing blows. He aimed for the gaps in the murmillo's armour—small, precise strikes that forced Draconis to adjust his stance.

The Turning Point

As the fight wore on, both men began to show signs of exhaustion. Sweat dripped into Rufus's eyes, stinging as he squinted against the sun's glare. Draconis's movements, once fluid and aggressive, became slower, more deliberate.

Rufus saw his moment. Feigning a stumble, he lured Draconis into stepping onto a patch of loose sand. The murmillo lunged, his massive shield raised, but his footing faltered as the unstable ground shifted beneath him.

Seizing the opportunity, Rufus darted forward, driving the edge of his shield into Draconis's exposed knee. The murmillo buckled, and the crowd roared as the invincible champion fell to one knee.

The Final Strike

Draconis wasn't finished. With a roar of fury, he swung his sword in a wide arc, forcing Rufus to leap backward. But the champion's movements were desperate now, lacking the precision that had defined the earlier stages of the fight.

Rufus moved in for the kill. He dodged another wild swing, closed the distance, and delivered a decisive blow to the murmillo's sword arm. Draconis's sword clattered to the sand, and for the first time, the crowd fell silent.

Rufus stood over his fallen opponent, his chest heaving, his sword poised. He could end it now. The murmillo's life was in his hands, and the crowd awaited his decision.

But as Rufus looked into Draconis's eyes, he saw something unexpected: not arrogance or defiance, but acceptance. This was a man who had given everything to the arena, who had lived and fought by its rules.

Rufus lowered his sword.

Redemption Earned

The crowd's silence turned into a deafening roar of approval, their cheers reverberating through the arena. Rufus raised his sword in salute—not just to the crowd, but to Draconis, who nodded in quiet acknowledgment as he was helped to his feet.

Back in the holding area, the lanista approached Rufus, his expression unreadable. "You've done what few ever could," he said. "You fought like a true champion. And now, you've earned your freedom."

The words hit Rufus like a wave. Freedom. For so long, it had been an abstract concept, something distant and almost unimaginable. Now, it was his.

As he stepped out of the ludus for the final time, Rufus paused, looking back at the walls that had contained so much of his pain and growth. The scars on his body felt lighter, less like burdens and more like badges of honour.

The road ahead was uncertain, but for the first time, it was his to choose. And as the sun dipped low in the sky, Rufus walked forward, his gladius at his side, ready to face whatever battles the future might hold.

Self-Help Lessons: The Final Fight – Earning Redemption

The air in the arena was electric, thick with the anticipation of the crowd. Rufus stood at the threshold of his greatest challenge yet, his grip tight on the sword that felt like an extension of his arm. The opponent before him wasn't just a towering murmillo with an unbeaten record—it was the embodiment of every doubt, every failure, and every sacrifice he had endured. This wasn't just a fight for survival; it was a fight for redemption.

The Fight That Defined Him

Rufus's path to this moment had been anything but easy. Every scar on his body told a story—a lesson learned, a setback overcome. He had trained relentlessly, transforming his weaknesses into strengths, but what set him apart wasn't just his skill. It was his unyielding resilience, forged in the fires of the ludus.

As the trumpet blared and the murmillo advanced, Rufus felt the weight of his journey settle on his shoulders. The murmillo's strikes were powerful, calculated, and unrelenting, but Rufus had learned to adapt. He anticipated the murmillo's moves, deflecting blows and looking for an opening. Each clash of steel was a reminder of the countless hours he'd spent honing his craft, of every moment he'd refused to give up when giving up would have been easier.

Relating Rufus's Fight to Everyday Battles

Rufus's struggle resonates with the battles we all face in life. Maybe it's the fear of failure when starting a new career, the overwhelming challenge of pursuing a degree while balancing a job, or the daunting task of rebuilding after personal loss. These moments, like Rufus's final fight, test our resolve and push us to grow.

Consider Sarah, a single mother who decided to return to school after a decade of working low-paying jobs. Balancing classes, work, and parenthood felt impossible at first, but she broke her goal into manageable steps—one course at a time, one late-night study session after another. There were setbacks: a failed exam, a missed deadline. But each time, Sarah picked herself up and adjusted her strategy. When she finally walked across the graduation stage, it wasn't just the degree she celebrated—it was the resilience and grit she'd built along the way.

Victory Through Preparation and Perspective

As Rufus's opponent faltered, caught off-guard by a well-timed feint, Rufus saw his opening. He struck, not with rage or desperation, but with precision born of discipline. The murmillo stumbled, disarmed and defeated, and the crowd erupted into cheers.

Standing in the centre of the arena, sword raised high, Rufus felt something deeper than triumph: peace. The fight had tested every fibre of his being, but it also reminded him that success isn't about the final blow—it's about the journey. Every setback, every gruelling training session, and every act of courage had brought him to this moment.

Self-Help Lessons: Preparing for Your Greatest Challenges

Rufus's story isn't just about a gladiator's victory; it's about how preparation, resilience, and the ability to adapt can lead to personal freedom and mastery. These lessons apply to any significant goal or challenge in life.

---

1. Major Goals Require Consistent Effort

Great achievements are rarely the result of sudden brilliance. They come from the accumulation of small, consistent efforts over time. Rufus didn't become a champion in a day—his journey was marked by persistence and discipline, even when progress felt slow.

In your life, whether you're building a career, improving your health, or nurturing a relationship, focus on the process. Each small step adds up, and the effort you invest today lays the foundation for tomorrow's success.

---

2. Setbacks Contribute to Success

Every failure Rufus endured taught him something valuable, from refining his strategy to deepening his resolve. Similarly, setbacks in your own life aren't the end—they're opportunities to grow stronger and smarter.

For example, Thomas Edison famously viewed his many failed attempts at creating the lightbulb as steps toward success, saying, "I have not failed. I've just found 10,000 ways that won't work." Reframing failure as part of the journey helps you stay focused on your ultimate goal.

---

3. Celebrate Progress Along the Way

Victory isn't just the final result—it's every milestone that gets you closer to your goal. Rufus's small victories in training gave him the confidence to face the murmillo. In your life, acknowledging progress keeps you motivated and reminds you of your growth.

Whether it's finishing a project, hitting a fitness milestone, or simply getting through a tough week, take time to celebrate. These moments reinforce your resilience and build momentum.

Practical Exercise: Planning for Victory

Here's how to prepare for your own "arena moments" with clarity and focus.

---

1. Write Your "Victory Plan"

Think about a significant goal you want to achieve. Write it down, then break it into smaller, actionable steps. **Example:**

- **Goal:** Save for a dream vacation.
- **Steps:**

1. Create a monthly savings plan.
2. Reduce non-essential expenses.
3. Research affordable travel options.

Having a clear plan turns an overwhelming goal into manageable actions.

---

2. Take the First Step

Identify the first step in your plan and commit to completing it this week.

Example: If your goal is to improve your fitness, start with a 10-minute daily walk.

Action creates momentum, reinforcing your commitment to the larger goal.

---

3. Reflect and Celebrate Progress

Set milestones within your plan and reward yourself when you reach them.

Example: After saving for three months, treat yourself to a small reward, like a dinner out or a new book.

Celebrating progress keeps you motivated and reminds you that every step forward is a victory.

The Takeaway

Rufus's final fight wasn't just about defeating an opponent—it was about proving to himself that every setback, every scar, and every lesson had prepared him for this moment. Your own victories will come the same way—not through luck, but through perseverance, preparation, and the courage to rise when it matters most.

So, step into your arena with confidence. The journey won't always be easy, but every step you take, every challenge you face, and every victory you celebrate will bring you closer to the life you've dreamed of.

Joke:

What did Rufus say before stepping into his final fight?

"If I survive this, I'm retiring to a nice quiet life—maybe as a barber. I've got plenty of experience with close shaves!"

The Gladiator Challenge: Claim Your Victory

Victory Plan: Write down one major goal and break it into actionable steps. Share your plan or your first small victory with #VictoryPlan.

Celebrate Progress: Post about a recent achievement and how it reflects your journey. Use #EarnYourRudis.

Final Reflection

The journey to achieving a major goal is never easy, but it is always worth it. Rufus's final fight wasn't just about defeating his opponent—it was about proving to himself that every moment of effort, every setback, and every scar had prepared him for that moment.

As you prepare for your own challenges, remember that success is built on consistent effort and the willingness to face obstacles with determination. Celebrate your progress, honour your journey, and trust that each step brings you closer to victory.

The arena awaits, and your moment to rise is here. Will you take the first step?

Chapter 11:

Freedom Earned – The Path Forward

The roar of the crowd was a distant echo now, fading into memory as Rufus walked through the gates of the arena for the last time. The rudis—a simple, unassuming wooden sword—was clutched tightly in his hand, its weight far lighter than the burden it symbolised. It marked his freedom, his triumph, and the end of a journey defined by blood, sweat, and unyielding resolve. Yet, as he stepped into the golden light of the setting sun, freedom felt heavier than any chain he had worn.

A Moment of Triumph

Rufus paused just beyond the arena walls, taking a deep breath of air untainted by the sweat and dust of combat. He ran his thumb over the smooth grain of the rudis, its simplicity almost mocking the complexity of emotions coursing through him. Victory, yes, but also loss. For years, the arena had been his world—a brutal, unforgiving world, but one that had shaped him into the man he was. What did freedom mean now, without the rhythm of training, the roar of the crowd, and the camaraderie forged in the fires of shared struggle?

His body, marked by countless scars, bore the story of his survival. Each jagged line was a memory: of triumph, of failure, of lessons learned the hard way. His mind, though sharpened by discipline and strategy, was crowded with faces—friends, rivals, mentors, and the fallen. The rudis represented a new beginning, but the past refused to loosen its grip.

Bittersweet Farewells

That evening, Rufus gathered with his closest allies in the ludus for one final meal. The air was thick with unspoken emotions as they sat around a modest table, the flickering light of the torches casting long shadows on the walls. Felix, ever the jokester, raised his goblet with a crooked grin.

"To Rufus," he said, "the man who made me look good by comparison."

Laughter rippled through the group, but it was tinged with melancholy. Castor, the young gladiator Rufus had once saved in the arena, lifted his own cup, his voice steady but his eyes shimmering with unshed tears.

"To the man who showed us what courage really looks like."

Marcus, who had once been more rival than friend, spoke last. His tone was quieter, more reflective. "To freedom," he said, holding Rufus's gaze. "And to the cost of earning it."

They drank, their cups clinking softly in the dim light. Rufus looked around at the faces that had become his family. Each bore their own scars, their own stories of survival and resilience. This was the hardest part—leaving behind the people who had stood by him in the arena, who had fought and bled alongside him. Freedom, he realized, was as much about what you leave behind as what lies ahead.

A Final Reckoning

Before he departed the ludus for good, Rufus sought out the lanista. The man stood in his office, surrounded by the trophies of his trade—helmets, swords, and the occasional rudis mounted on the walls. He turned as Rufus entered, his expression unreadable.

"So," the lanista said, his voice as sharp as ever. "You've earned your freedom. I suppose congratulations are in order."

Rufus studied the man who had shaped his life in ways both cruel and necessary. The lanista had been his tormentor and his teacher, the architect of his suffering and his survival. "You taught me to endure," Rufus said at last. "For that, I thank you. But you also made me a weapon, and for that, I can't forgive you."

The lanista's lips twitched, almost forming a smile. "Forgiveness isn't necessary. You were a good investment, Rufus, but you became more than that. You proved me wrong. That doesn't happen often."

There was a pause, heavy with the weight of unspoken truths. Finally, the lanista extended his hand. "Good luck out there. Freedom isn't the end—it's the beginning."

Rufus hesitated, then clasped the man's hand. It was not a gesture of reconciliation but of closure, a final chapter written in their shared history.

The Road Ahead

As Rufus walked away from the ludus, the world stretched out before him like a blank canvas. The open road was daunting, filled with uncertainties and challenges he could only begin to imagine. Yet, for the first time, he was the master of his own fate.

He thought of the young gladiators he had mentored, their eager faces and the lessons he had passed on. He resolved to use his experiences—not as a burden, but as a gift. The scars he carried, once symbols of pain and survival, would now serve as marks of wisdom and growth.

Freedom, Rufus realized, was not the absence of struggle but the ability to choose one's battles. And he would choose to fight for others—not with swords and shields, but with guidance and strength. The arena had forged him into a warrior, but life beyond its walls would define the man he would become.

With the rudis tucked into his belt, Rufus stepped onto the dusty road, his gaze fixed on the horizon. The past was behind him, but its lessons would guide his every step. The future was unwritten, but Rufus was ready to meet it head-on, armed with the resilience, courage, and adaptability that had carried him this far.

The journey was far from over, but for the first time, it was his to write.

Historical Context: The Complex Nature of Gladiatorial Freedom

For freed gladiators, life after the arena was often uncertain. Many, like Rufus, bore the physical and psychological scars of their battles. Some chose to leave the world of combat behind, embracing quiet lives as farmers, artisans, or trainers. Others returned to the arena as *auctorati*, voluntarily fighting for wealth or glory, unable to resist the call of the sand and the crowd.

Freed gladiators who turned to mentorship often found a sense of purpose, using their hard-won knowledge to guide younger fighters. Their stories served as both warnings and inspirations, proving that survival was possible, even in the harshest of conditions.

Reflection

Rufus's journey from a captive to a champion and finally to a free man is a testament to the human spirit's capacity for resilience and growth. His scars tell the story of battles fought and lessons learned, but it is his choices—his decision to act with integrity, to lead, and to embrace his freedom—that define his legacy.

Freedom is not the absence of struggle but the ability to shape your own destiny. Like Rufus, we all face our own arenas, our own battles for redemption and purpose. And when the gates finally open, it is up to us to walk forward, carrying the lessons of our past into a future we have the power to create.

The horizon is yours to claim. What will you do with your freedom?

Self-Help Lessons: The Arena of Life

Life is its own arena. Every day, we face challenges that test our resilience, choices that define our character, and opportunities that shape our future. The story of Rufus isn't just an epic tale of gladiatorial triumph—it's a metaphor for the battles we all fight.

His journey from captivity to freedom mirrors the universal struggle to overcome setbacks, discover our strengths, and leave a meaningful legacy.

Defining True Freedom

When Rufus walked out of the ludus, his scars didn't fade, nor did his memories vanish. But those scars were no longer marks of defeat—they were symbols of his survival and growth. True freedom, Rufus realized, is not about the absence of hardship but about mastering oneself. It's about turning pain into purpose and using the lessons of the past to shape the future.

We all carry our own versions of scars, whether from personal losses, professional challenges, or emotional battles. These marks are not chains; they're proof of our resilience. They remind us that freedom isn't given—it's earned by confronting our fears, learning from our failures, and staying true to our values.

Leadership Through Service

Rufus's greatest triumph wasn't just his victory in the arena; it was the way he lifted others. By mentoring younger gladiators and leading by example, he turned his struggles into tools for their success.

In our own lives, true success lies not in individual achievement but in helping others grow. Whether it's offering guidance to a colleague, teaching a skill, or supporting a loved one, sharing what we've learned creates ripples that extend far beyond ourselves. It transforms personal growth into a legacy of resilience and connection.

Embracing Change

Walking away from the ludus wasn't easy for Rufus. The arena, with all its hardships, had shaped him. But he knew that growth required stepping into the unknown. Leaving behind the comfort of the familiar—whether it's a job, a relationship, or even an old mindset—is daunting, but it's also where transformation happens.

As you face your own transitions, remember that every ending is also a beginning. By carrying the lessons of your past into your next chapter, you honour where you've been while creating space for who you're becoming.

Call to Action: A 30-Day Growth Challenge

Freedom and mastery are built one step at a time. Use this 30-day challenge to apply the lessons of Rufus's journey to your own life.

Week 1: Self-Awareness

Focus on understanding yourself—your values, strengths, and areas for growth.

- **Day 1:** Write down your core values and what they mean to you.
- **Day 2:** Reflect on a recent challenge and how you handled it. What did you learn?
- **Day 3:** Identify one fear that's holding you back. Write down three small steps to face it.

Week 2: Building Resilience

Cultivate habits and mindsets that help you stay strong in adversity.

- **Day 8:** Start a "small wins" journal. Each day, record one thing you did well.
- **Day 10:** Practice mindfulness for five minutes—focus on your breathing or simply observe your thoughts.
- **Day 12:** Reflect on a setback and list three lessons you learned from it.

Week 3: Strengthening Connections

Invest in the relationships that support and inspire you.

- **Day 15:** Reach out to someone who has positively impacted your life. Express your gratitude.
- **Day 17:** Identify one person you can support. Plan an action to help them this week.
- **Day 20:** Reflect on a time when someone helped you. What did their support mean to you?

Week 4: Legacy and Purpose

Focus on how you can use your journey to make a difference.

- **Day 22:** Write down one area where you can mentor or guide others.
- **Day 25:** Plan a small act of service—help a friend, volunteer, or share your knowledge.
- **Day 30:** Reflect on the past month. What did you learn about yourself? How will you carry these lessons forward?

The Arena Awaits

Like Rufus, you are both the gladiator and the master of your own fate. The battles you face today are not the end—they are the proving grounds for the victories yet to come. Your scars, your struggles, and your triumphs are all part of the story you're writing.

Step into your arena with courage, resilience, and purpose. The path ahead may not be easy, but it is yours to define. Will you rise to the challenge? The choice is yours.

The rudis is in your hand. The arena awaits.

Joke:

What did Rufus say when someone called him a gladiator after his freedom?

"Actually, I'm a freelance survival expert now."

The Gladiator Challenge: Step Into Your Freedom

Freedom Speech: Write a short "freedom speech" reflecting on your journey through the book and what you've learned. Post it with #MyRudis.

Ultimate Challenge: Create a montage of your journey through these challenges—photos, videos, or a written summary. Use #GladiatorChallengeUltimate and encourage others to join.

Final Reflection

Freedom is not a destination—it is a journey. It is not the absence of struggle but the presence of choice, resilience, and purpose. Rufus's story reminds us that true freedom comes from within, from mastering your fears, embracing your scars, and using your experiences to shape a meaningful path forward.

Your journey may not involve the sands of the arena, but it carries the same lessons. Every battle you've fought, every challenge you've overcome, has prepared you for this moment. As you step into your own freedom, remember that the choices you make now will define not just your life but the lives of those you inspire.

Who will you become? The rudis is in your hands.

Conclusion: The Arena of Life

Life stretches before us like the vast sands of an arena, unpredictable and relentless. Each day brings its own battles—some are external, like the demands of work or the weight of responsibilities; others are internal, waged against fear, doubt, or the shadows of past failures. Yet, as Rufus has shown us, the true measure of strength lies not in the absence of struggle but in the resilience to rise, to fight, and to grow.

The arena may be unforgiving, but it is also where champions are forged. With every challenge comes an opportunity to discover who you are and what you are capable of. The battles you face are not there to break you but to reveal your strength, sharpen your character, and prepare you for the victories ahead.

Inspirational Message: Lessons from Rufus's Journey

Rufus's story is not just a tale of survival; it is a mirror for the struggles we all face. His journey through the brutality of the arena, his battle to trust again, to adapt, to lead, and to find freedom, is a testament to the power of resilience and the choices that define us. His scars, both physical and emotional, did not diminish him—they empowered him. They were reminders of his courage, his adaptability, and his unyielding spirit.

In your own life, you may face setbacks that feel insurmountable, moments where the weight of the world presses down and defeat feels inevitable. But remember this: it is not the obstacles that define you—it is your response to them. Every scar, every failure, every hard-fought victory is a chapter in your story, proof that you have faced the arena and chosen to fight.

Freedom, as Rufus discovered, is not the absence of struggle. It is the ability to face it head-on, with strength, integrity, and the knowledge that you are more than the sum of your battles. True freedom comes from mastering yourself, from understanding that you hold the rudis—the symbol of your power to shape your destiny.

Call to Action: Embrace Your Inner Gladiator

The lessons Rufus learned in the arena are not his alone. They belong to all of us. His journey has shown that resilience, discipline, and courage are not extraordinary qualities—they are within us all, waiting to be awakened. Now it's your turn to step into the sands of your own arena, to face your battles with the strength of a gladiator.

1. **Start Small: Take Action Today**

Choose one lesson or exercise from this book that resonated with you. Maybe it's committing to a new habit, reflecting on a setback, or reaching out to someone in your network. Every small step is a victory, a move toward becoming the person you aspire to be.

2. **Keep Momentum: Track Your Progress**

Growth isn't a single moment—it's a journey. Use a journal to document your challenges, your breakthroughs, and the lessons you gather along the way. Share your story with a trusted friend or join the #GladiatorChallenge community to inspire others and find inspiration in return.

3. **Embrace Growth: See Challenges as Stepping Stones**

Every challenge you face is an opportunity to grow. Like Rufus, approach each battle with strategy, courage, and an open mind. Remember that even setbacks are part of the journey, shaping you into a stronger, wiser version of yourself.

The Arena Awaits

Rufus's story has come to an end, but yours is just beginning. Life's arena is not a place of defeat—it is a proving ground for greatness. It is where you face the struggles that define you, where you discover your strengths and your purpose. The journey ahead will test you, but it will also transform you.

Go forth, not with fear, but with determination and heart. Step into your battles with the confidence of a gladiator who has trained for this very moment. Like Rufus, you already possess the courage, the resilience, and the wisdom to rise, to fight, and to triumph.

The rudis is in your hands now—a symbol of your freedom, your power, and your potential. The choice is yours. Will you rise?

Ready for Your Next Transformation? Explore More by Rowan X. Adler!

Conquer the World: How to Overcome Insurmountable Obstacles
Discover the timeless lessons of Scipio Africanus and learn how to turn setbacks into opportunities for victory. Packed with ancient wisdom and modern strategies, this book will inspire you to rise above life's challenges and forge your path to greatness.

Rise from the Arena: A Gladiator's Guide to Overcoming Life's Greatest Challenges

Step into the sandals of a Roman gladiator and uncover powerful insights on resilience, discipline, and triumph. This unique blend of storytelling and actionable advice will empower you to face your toughest battles with honour and strength.

Productivity and Time Management

Reclaim your time, master your focus, and design a life you love with this approachable guide. From conquering distractions to building habits that stick, this book is your roadmap to achieving more with ease.

Personal Growth and Self-Improvement

Embark on a journey of self-discovery with this empowering guide to unlocking your potential. Whether you're building resilience, breaking bad habits, or finding clarity, this book will help you take the first steps toward lasting change.

Motivation and Goal Setting

Turn your dreams into reality with practical tools to ignite your motivation and craft achievable goals. This book is perfect for anyone ready to overcome procrastination, build confidence, and stay on track.

Mindfulness Made Simple

Discover how small, mindful changes can lead to big transformations. With relatable stories and step-by-step exercises, this book will help you find peace, focus, and joy in the chaos of everyday life.

Simplify Your Day: Easy Time Management Tips for Success
Learn how to work smarter, not harder, with practical time management tips that fit seamlessly into your busy life. This book is your key to balancing productivity and personal fulfilment.

📖 **Explore all of Rowan X. Adler's books and start your next transformation today! Visit www.rowanxadler.com for more inspiration, free resources, and updates on upcoming releases.**

✨ **Your journey doesn't end here—it's only the beginning. Take the next step today!**

www.ingramcontent.com/pod-product-compliance
Lightning Source LLC
LaVergne TN
LVHW050559160826
845677LV00011B/2367

* 9 7 9 8 2 3 0 8 9 4 6 8 1 *